CYRUS
THE
GREAT

CYRUS THE GREAT

CONQUEROR, LIBERATOR, ANOINTED ONE

STEPHEN DANDO-COLLINS

WITH AN AFTERWORD BY
PROFESSOR DAVID RICHTER

Turner Publishing Company
Nashville, Tennessee
www.turnerpublishing.com

Cyrus the Great

Cover design: Alex Merto
Book design: Erin Seaward-Hiatt

Library of Congress Cataloging-in-Publication Data
Names: Dando-Collins, Stephen, author.
Title: Cyrus the Great : conqueror, liberator, anointed one / Stephen Dando-Collins.

Other titles: Conqueror, liberator, anointed one
Description: [Nashville] : Turner Publishing Company, [2020] | Includes
  bibliographical references and index. | Summary: "Cyrus the Great was
  one of the most influential figures in history, an enlightened ruler and
  brilliant general who created the Persian Empire, the largest empire
  known to man to that time. This concise and telling biography is the
  first of its kind for Cyrus, and especially relevant since the 2016
  presidential election."-- Provided by publisher.
Identifiers: LCCN 2019035585 (print) | LCCN 2019035586 (ebook) | ISBN
  9781684424375 (paperback) | ISBN 9781684424382 (hardcover) | ISBN
  9781684424399 (ebook)
Subjects: LCSH: Cyrus, the Great, King of Persia, -530 B.C. or 529 B.C. |
  Iran--Kings and rulers--Biography. | Iran--History--To 640.
Classification: LCC DS282 .D36 2020 (print) | LCC DS282 (ebook) | DDC
  935/.05092 [B]--dc23
LC record available at https://lccn.loc.gov/2019035585
LC ebook record available at https://lccn.loc.gov/2019035586

Printed in the United States of America

17 18 19 20 10 9 8 7 6 5 4 3 2 1

"I AM CYRUS,

KING OF THE WORLD,

GREAT KING, POWERFUL KING,

KING OF BABYLON, KING OF SUMER AND AKKAD,

KING OF THE FOUR QUARTERS OF THE EARTH,

SON OF CAMBYSES, GREAT KING, KING OF ANSHAN,

DESCENDANT OF TEISPES, GREAT KING, KING OF ANSHAN,

THE PERPETUAL SEED OF KINGSHIP,

WHOSE REIGN BEL AND NABU LOVE.

"

THE CYRUS CYLINDER, BABYLON, 538 BC

"God protect this country from foe, famine, and falsehood."

—DARIUS THE GREAT, third successor to Cyrus the Great, king of Persia, from an inscription at Persepolis

With grateful thanks to my New York literary agent, Richard Curtis, for his guidance; to my publisher, Stephanie Beard, for her support; to Professor David Richter for his learned Afterword; and to my anointed one, my wife, Louise, for her everlasting love.

CITY OF BABYLON, 539 B.C.
AT THE TIME OF CYRUS' PERSIAN ASSAULT

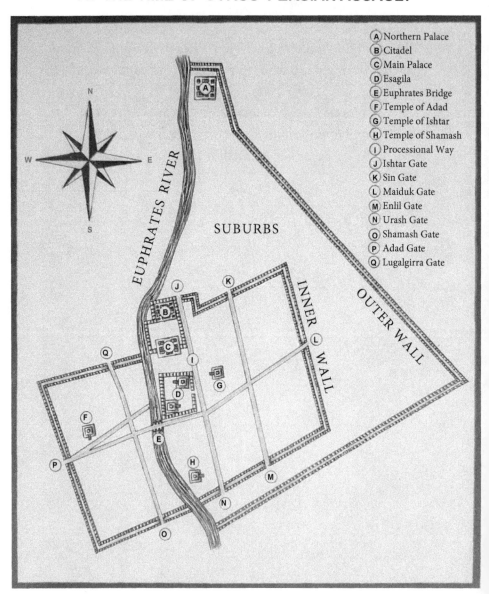

A. Northern Palace
B. Citadel
C. Main Palace
D. Esagila
E. Euphrates Bridge
F. Temple of Adad
G. Temple of Ishtar
H. Temple of Shamash
I. Processional Way
J. Ishtar Gate
K. Sin Gate
L. Maiduk Gate
M. Enlil Gate
N. Urash Gate
O. Shamash Gate
P. Adad Gate
Q. Lugalgirra Gate

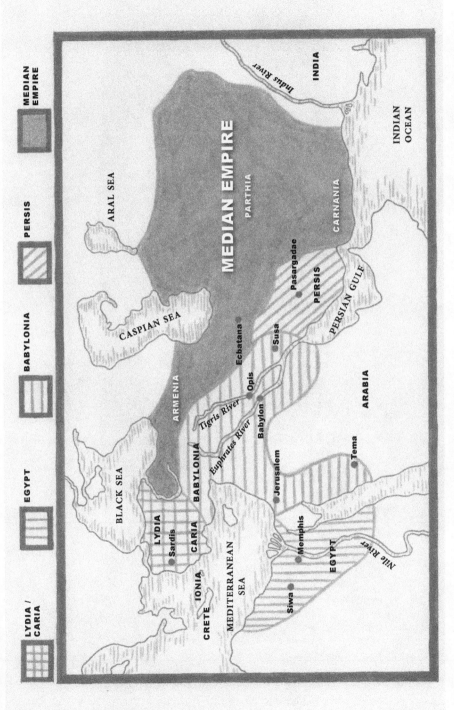

STATE OF ANCIENT WORLD AT START OF CYRUS' REVOLT AGAINST MEDIA, 552 B.C.

#1. Cyrus the Great as depicted on the Cyrus Stele at Pasargadae.
(Photograph: John Wright.)

#2. Greek amphora showing the fabulously rich King Croesus of Lydia on a pyre being lit by a Persian soldier following the fall of Sardis to Cyrus's army. *Photograph: Bibi Saint-Pol.*

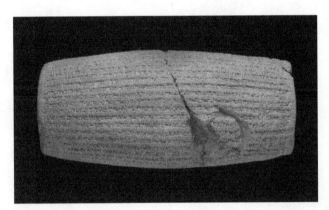

#3. The Cyrus Cylinder. *Courtesy of the British Museum.*

#4. A commemorative coin depicting Cyrus the Great and US President Donald Trump, issued by a religious group in 2018.

TABLE OF CONTENTS

INTRODUCTION: Our Sources on Cyrus | 1

CHAPTER 1: Kill the Child | 11

CHAPTER 2: Deporting the Jews to Babylon | 19

CHAPTER 3: The Boy in the Basket | 23

CHAPTER 4: Saved by the Magi | 30

CHAPTER 5: Jerusalem Destroyed | 34

CHAPTER 6: In the Court of the King | 37

CHAPTER 7: Leading the Persian Revolt | 43

CHAPTER 8: Cyrus's First Battle | 50

CHAPTER 9: Battle of the Border | 58

CHAPTER 10: Battle of Pasargadae: The Fall of Astyages | 64

CHAPTER 11: A Mighty Empire Will Be Destroyed | 72

CHAPTER 12: Croesus Versus Cyrus | 77

CHAPTER 13: Sardis: The Fallen Helmet | 88

CHAPTER 14: Killing a King | 96

CHAPTER 15: Feet of Clay | 108

CHAPTER 16: Marching on Babylon | 121

CHAPTER 17: The Writing Is on the Wall for Nabonidus | 136

CHAPTER 18: Cyrus Frees the Jews of Babylon | 146

CHAPTER 19: "Do Not Grudge Me My Monument" | 159

CHAPTER 20: The Sons of Cyrus | 164

CHAPTER 21: Darius and the Jerusalem Temple | 177

EPILOGUE: Was Cyrus Great? And Is There a Modern Parallel? | 183

AFTERWORD | 189

ENDNOTES | 207

BIBLIOGRAPHY | 214

INDEX | 217

INTRODUCTION

Our Sources on Cyrus

C YRUS THE GREAT was one of the most influential figures in history, an enlightened ruler and brilliant general who, via sword, cunning, and wisdom, in the sixth century BC created the Persian Empire, the largest empire known to man at that time. His army was based around one of the most famous bodyguard units in history, the Immortals, which until Cyrus's death, was unbeaten in battle.

Cyrus was magnanimous toward captured enemies and freed peoples enslaved by King Nebuchadnezzar II, sending them back to their homelands. He is most famous for freeing the Jews held at Babylon, after Cyrus's troops overran the city, and allowing them to return to Jerusalem. According to Jewish tradition, not only did Cyrus also give the Jews back the artifacts that Nebuchadnezzar had looted from their temple, he gave permission and provided funds for the Second Temple's construction. In Jewish and Christian texts, Cyrus was chosen by God to free the Jews and help them rebuild the temple, becoming the only non-Jew described in the Old Testament as "anointed" by God.

Cyrus has been credited with being the originator of a human rights creed that influenced Thomas Jefferson and his contribution to the United States Bill of Rights. Jefferson not only had a copy of the *Cyropaedia* of Greek writer Xenophon of Athens, a book in which the words, thoughts, and experiences of Cyrus are expounded, but he also made copious notations in the margins. Many other politicians, including Italy's duplicitous Niccolò Machiavelli, drew inspiration from Cyrus and the *Cyropaedia*. But how reliable is Xenophon's book?

Xenophon lived more than a century after Cyrus. He commanded Greek mercenary troops in the Persian army of another Cyrus—called Cyrus the Younger by historians—who staged an unsuccessful military coup that aimed to overthrow his elder brother, the Persian king Artaxerxes II. Like Plato, Xenophon was a student of Greek philosopher Socrates, and he claimed to have been told by Socrates and Plato much of what he wrote about Cyrus, and there are clear and frequent examples of Xenophon putting Socratic words in the mouth of Cyrus.

The *Cyropaedia* reads like a fairy tale, often bearing little resemblance to known facts about Cyrus and other figures of his time. Xenophon clearly invented numerous characters. He also killed off Cyrus's Median grandfather Astyages early in the piece, when all other sources have Astyages living considerably longer. And Xenophon gave Astyages a son named Cyaxares, making him Cyrus's uncle, chief lieutenant, and confidant, when we know that Astyages had no son at all, and Cyaxares was Astyages's father, who died when Cyrus was a teenager.

Xenophon also made basic historical errors, including crediting Cyrus with conquering Egypt; that would in fact be accomplished by Cyrus's son Cambyses II after Cyrus's death. Xenophon wrote of Persian nobles worshipping the principal Mesopotamian god Mithra, or Bel as he was generally known, but portrayed Cyrus worshipping and sacrificing to the gods of the Greek pantheon, which, from inscriptions, we know to be wholly untrue; Cyrus also worshipped Bel. Xenophon seems to have done this to make Cyrus more acceptable to his Greek readers. Xenophon also frequently gave incorrect place names, and his chronology was sometimes inaccurate. Occasionally, too, it's possible to see where Xenophon borrowed from Herodotus (who is discussed below).

Scholars have long remarked that Xenophon's descriptions of Cyrus growing up in Persia are obviously based on the Spartan king Agesilaus II and Sparta's strict military customs; Xenophon befriended and served Agesilaus. Many scholars believe that other aspects of Cyrus's youth that Xenophon wrote about are actually based on Xenophon's own youth. Xenophon most noticeably created long philosophical conversations and speeches and put them in the mouths of Cyrus and others. He never claimed to be writing history, and clearly his intent was to write an adventure story that showed off his own worldly wisdom, using historical figures such as Cyrus as his mouthpiece. As John Percival, Bishop of Hereford, very correctly observes in an introduction to an edition of the *Cyropaedia*, Xenophon's book is "a political romance."[1]

Further confirmation that Xenophon was prone to invention comes in his *Apology of Socrates to the Jury*, which covers the trial of Socrates at Athens that preceded the philosopher's 399 BC death. Xenophon gives the words and thoughts of Socrates, even though he wasn't present and never spoke to Socrates himself during or following the trial. Xenophon wasn't even in Athens at the time.

Demonstrably then, Xenophon is one of the least reliable historical sources on Cyrus. It's ironic that the content of America's Bill of Rights was in part inspired by the inventions of a novel. Only Xenophon's description of Persian military customs—customs which he claimed were handed down by Cyrus and which he witnessed firsthand a century after Cyrus's death—can be reasonably considered to have some basis in fact, along with, perhaps, several observations about Cyrus's leadership style, which accord with other accounts of Cyrus's life.

Meanwhile, facing Xenophon and his fellow Greek mercenaries at the Battle of Cunaxa in 401 BC was the Greek doctor Ctesias, who was on the staff of Persian king Artaxerxes II. From Cnidus in Caria, then part of the Persian Empire, Ctesias dressed a nonfatal chest wound received by King Artaxerxes in the battle. Ctesias served in the king's court for as long as seventeen years and later wrote a history of Assyria/Babylon and Persia called the *Persica*, which he claimed to have based on material he found in the royal Persian archives.

By the first century AD, Ctesias was being ridiculed by Greco-Roman author Plutarch (discussed below), who described Ctesias's work as "a perfect farrago of incredible and senseless fables."[2] Modern historians also cast doubt on the accuracy of Ctesias in many respects, principally because his account frequently differs from the history recorded on inscriptions unearthed in recent times.

Ctesias also gave incorrect names to various historical figures or placed them in the wrong era. Most notably, he called Cyrus's father "Atredates." He also made both Cyrus's parents Persians and members of the minor Mardi tribe. Herodotus, and Cyrus's own words on the Cyrus Cylinder and his later establishment of the Persian capital in the territory of the Pasargadae tribe, leave us in no doubt that Cyrus's father was Cambyses, a member of the Achaemenid clan of the Pasargadae. Ctesias also wrongly named Cyrus's foster parents, and he seemingly invented numerous other characters for dramatic effect and story exposition.

Ctesias derided the histories of another Greek author and native of Caria who wrote about Cyrus some forty years before Ctesias, Herodotus of Halicarnassus. Ctesias claimed that his own work offered the true and accurate account of the history of Persia, and at times the influence of Herodotus on Ctesias is clear, where Ctesias deliberately took episodes from Herodotus and gave them to other characters in the *Persica*, often with nonsensical results.

It just goes to show that professional jealousy existed between authors as far back as 2,500 years ago.

While Ctesias described Herodotus as a "maker of fables," Herodotus was described by Roman author Cicero as "the Father of History," and today Herodotus is widely considered the first genuine historian, while it's Ctesias who is rated the maker of fables. For example, Roman author Arrian (discussed below) described Ctesias's work as nonsense.

Nonetheless, some of the content of Ctesias's *Persica* does help to explain various events and characteristics, and fill in gaps, in the lives of Cyrus and other historical figures, including his chief lieutenant Oebares and King Croesus of Lydia, and it occasionally has a ring of truth about it, suggesting a sometimes factual basis. For instance, Ctesias gives us the only detailed accounts of Cyrus's battles against King Astyages of Media that led to Cyrus defeating the Median army, capturing the Median capital Ecbatana, and making Astyages a prisoner. Here the information he offers doesn't conflict with other sources but rather fills it out.

Lloyd Llewellyn-Jones, editor of a modern English translation of the *Persica*, cautions against totally dismissing Ctesias's work. "Ctesias is often regarded as small-fry, a historian of little consequence," he writes. But, despite some clearly fantastical and unfounded elements in the *Persica*, Llewellyn-Jones is of the opinion that "Ctesias can be read as a serious historian at times ... although one has to filter it through other literary genres that interweave throughout the narrative." Those other literary genres are fable and fiction.[3]

This brings us to Herodotus. A well-educated Greek, he traveled throughout the Greek and Persian worlds during his lifetime, observing the geography, nature, people, and customs of the regions and recording their human history as told to him by locals, putting it all on parchment in his twenty-three-book masterwork *The Histories*, which some accounts say he premiered with a live reading in the literary contest that then formed part of the Olympic Games.

Prior to Herodotus, history was imparted in inscriptions and orally in the form of narratives told by storytellers, usually in verse form, which contained large elements of fiction—Herodotus would even question whether the Trojan War took place as described by Homer. Herodotus broke with tradition and changed the concept of recording history by committing *The Histories* to written form, and in easy-to-read prose, which permitted anyone who could read to share his work and gain an insight into past people, places, and events.

Herodotus was the first to admit he sometimes received conflicting accounts about various people and events and was also told stories that had more to do with folklore and myth than established fact. He frankly wrote in *The Histories* that there were three accounts of Cyrus's childhood apart from the version that he felt closest to the truth and which he gave us. He sometimes related aspects of these alternative versions and explained why he chose one over another. This analytical approach is akin to the approach of most modern historians.

Nonetheless Herodotus was occasionally in error, sometimes with personal names, sometimes with descriptions of places, and he occasionally skipped over or omitted events that we know about from other sources. For example, he barely mentioned Cyrus's three battles on his way to conquering Media. It seems he edited out some battles as a matter of expediency rather than through ignorance of them. At other times, Herodotus's chronological order of events can be confused, and his placement of Cyrus in Persia, when he was secretly approached to launch his revolt against Median rule, is demonstrably incorrect, as will later be explained. Still, overall, Herodotus remains by far our most reliable source for the life and times of Cyrus the Great.

We have to move forward several centuries to the next author to offer new information on Cyrus. This was Nicolaus of Damascus.

Because he wrote a biography of Abraham, among his numerous works, and served Herod the Great, Jewish king of Judea, Nicolaus is believed to have himself been Jewish.

A learned first century BC teacher and writer from Syria, then a Roman province, Nicolaus served as tutor to the children of Mark Antony and his consort Queen Cleopatra of Egypt, then became friendly with Roman emperor Augustus, whose biography he also wrote. Augustus recommended Nicolaus's services to King Herod, who employed him as an adviser. Nicolaus wrote about Cyrus the Great, drawing heavily on Ctesias, offering interesting new pieces of information about Cyrus, which may or may not be true. Because few of his "facts" have been corroborated by other sources, Nicolaus's work on Cyrus has generally been considered by scholars to be fiction. However, some of his information does fill in gaps in Cyrus's story and offers logical explanations for some of his acts, so Nicolaus cannot be ignored.

Flavius Josephus was a Romano-Jewish historian of the first century. A former Jewish commander during the Jewish Revolt that led to the AD 70 Roman capture and destruction of Jerusalem, he switched sides and, with the emperors Vespasian and Titus as his patrons, wrote several histories of the Jews. In his *Jewish Antiquities*, he used existing sources, including biblical texts, Xenophon, and Berossus (discussed below) for his references to Cyrus and his decrees regarding the freeing of the Jews and rebuilding of the Temple at Jerusalem. Josephus also provided some detail about the fall of Jerusalem to Nebuchadnezzar immediately prior to Cyrus's reign.

Romano-Greek author Plutarch gives us interesting tidbits on Cyrus. Living in the first and second centuries AD, he was once considered a mere gossip writer. Today Plutarch is taken more seriously. An author and teacher from the Greek island of Boeotia who rose through the Roman civil service, Plutarch briefly referenced Cyrus when he wrote about Alexander the Great and gives us an interesting insight into King Croesus of Lydia leading up to his war with Cyrus. For many years, Plutarch served as one of the part-time priests administering the Temple of Apollo at Delphi, which entailed overseeing the delivery of the Pythia's monthly predictions at the temple. As you will see, the oracle of Delphi played an interesting part in the stories of Croesus and Cyrus.

Lucius Flavius Arrian, a Greek-born Roman senator, general, and provincial governor from Bithynia, lived at much the same time as Plutarch. Arrian wrote extensively, including a noted biography of Alexander the Great, and was called the Second Xenophon for his style and subjects. Arrian, in his *Anabasis*, tells of Alexander the Great's admiration of Cyrus and restoration of his tomb.

The Old Testament books of Daniel, Isaiah, Jeremiah, Esther, Kings, and Chronicles make reference to the Jewish exile to Babylon and specific reference to Cyrus allowing the Jews to return to Jerusalem, even referring to Cyrus as "anointed by God" to serve God's purposes. Daniel, believed by scholars such as Professor David Richter to have been written as much as 370 years after the events it describes (see Afterword), bounces around chronologically and contains numerous demonstrable historical errors. The book of Ezra, however, does offer insight into the famous decree of Cyrus. In addition, other Jewish works such as the Talmud provide clarification of some related aspects.

We have several Babylonian sources on Cyrus. One is the *Babyloniaca*, a history of Assyria/Babylonia by Berossus, a magus, or priest, of Marduk, the principal Babylonian deity. Berossus lived in Babylon about two hundred years after Cyrus, but in his important priestly role would have had access to official archives. His work was written in Greek, reflecting the fact that Babylon had by that time become part of the Macedonian empire created by Alexander the Great. Berossus wrote of Cyrus's conquest of Babylonia, and while the original has not come down to us, parts of the *Babyloniaca* were excerpted by Josephus in his *Jewish Antiquities*, and by other authors including Eusebius, Christian bishop of Caesarea, in his fourth century AD *Chronicon.*

Other Babylonian works to mention Cyrus are called collectively the Nabonidus Cylinders. Unearthed in modern times at centers including Babylon, Harran, and Sippar, several of these were created in the lifetime of Nabonidus, Babylon's last indigenous king, and at least one during the reign of Cyrus, and tell of Nabonidus's rule and the growing threat of his neighbor Cyrus. A further inscribed work, the Chronicle of Nabonidus, thought to have been the work of priestly magi of Marduk at Babylon during Cyrus's reign, was written on a baked clay tablet that is today in the British Museum and tells of the defeat of Nabonidus by Cyrus.

One of the most important and influential sources on Cyrus is the Cyrus Cylinder, which was unearthed in 1879 during excavation of Babylon's Esagila, the Great Temple, dedicated to Marduk. Today to be seen behind glass in the British Museum, the Cyrus Cylinder is an almost totally preserved baked-clay cylinder less than a foot (30 cm) long, covered with Akkadian (Babylonian) cuneiform script. With this cylinder, Cyrus was emulating previous kings of Babylon, including Nebuchadnezzar II.

The Cyrus Cylinder's text includes a self-propagandizing statement by Cyrus on how he conquered Babylon, restored the worship of Marduk, and repaired and improved the great city. It goes on to detail how, during the following year, Cyrus freed foreign captives who had been taken to Babylon by King Nebuchadnezzar half a century before and allowed them to return to their homelands and restore their old temples.

Many modern scholars and authors have also offered their thoughts on the life of Cyrus—among them the noted British science fiction writer H.G. Wells in his 1921 nonfiction work *The Outline of History*, a bestseller in its day—and are worth exploration.

These, then, are the sources for the life of Cyrus the Great: a mixture of legend and propaganda, conflicting histories and folk tales, biblical texts and archaeological discoveries, scholarly opinion and counter opinion. Using my experience in the fields of ancient military history and biography, I have taken the most credible—and where possible, verifiable—aspects of Cyrus's life from multiple sources and endeavored to piece them together to create a robust biography of the first king of the Persian Empire.

Noted American political biographer Robert Caro recently said that when it comes to truth in biography, "there is no truth." The best that a biographer can do, says Caro, is assemble as many facts as possible and "come close to the truth."[4] Caro has had the benefit of interviewing many living witnesses to the lives he documents. The problem with writing about someone who lived two and a half millennia ago is that there are no eyewitnesses to interview. In that case, sorting the fact from the fiction becomes even more difficult.

I can only say that the picture I have created of Cyrus on the following pages is the one I believe to be closest to the truth, based on the available information and based on, in the words of the philosopher Aristotle, "the resemblances" in the stories about Cyrus. (See the following chapter's references to divining dreams.) By this I mean that I have followed the common threads that run through his life—as recorded by multiple ancient sources.

This, then, is the story of King Cyrus the Great, as best that ancient sources and modern analysis will allow.

1

KILL THE CHILD

I N 600 BC OR THEREABOUTS, a son was born to the daughter of a prince. His birthplace was the royal palace in Ecbatana,
capital city of the Median Empire, which stretched across today's
Iran and eastern Turkey. The newborn child was immediately in
danger of losing his life. As you will shortly see, this was not for
medical reasons, but political.

Ecbatana, or the Gathering Place, sat on the gentle lower slopes
of Mount Alvand and today is the site of the city of Hamadan. Being
on the crossroads of east-west trade, Ecbatana was a prosperous city.
It must also have been a visually stunning city to behold. Seven con-
centric walls protected the population of Ecbatana, each wall taller
than the one that preceded it. The outermost wall was painted white,
the next black, the next scarlet, the next blue, the next orange. The
battlements of the sixth wall shone with silver, while those of the
innermost wall glowed with gold. This inner wall surrounded the
royal treasuries and the palace of the king of Media.

That king in 600 BC was Cyaxares, elderly descendant of two
soldier kings who had defeated their Assyrian overlords and

asserted Median independence. Even more warlike than his predecessors, King Cyaxares had expanded the Median Empire by applying superior military skills—he was reputedly the first ruler in Asia Minor to divide his army into distinct companies and separate the spearmen, archers, and cavalry.

His son Astyages, who would have been in his forties or fifties at this time, was a highly superstitious and paranoid prince who expected to soon succeed his aging father. In 601 BC, he'd had a wondrous dream in which water poured from his daughter Mandana—written as Mandane by Greek authors—and flooded Ecbatana before going on to flood all of Asia. Perplexed by this dream, Astyages summoned the leading magi to decipher it for him.

The magi were the priests of the Mesopotamian religion. We derive the word *magic* from the magi, whose name literally means "sorcerers." They were considered society's most learned men, being skilled mathematicians and astrologers. It was magi from Mesopotamia who followed the "star" from the east—identified as Halley's Comet by modern astrologers—in the story of the birth of Jesus Christ in the Christian gospel of Matthew. The Iranian city of Saveh proudly claims to have been the Median starting point and burial place of those three magi.

As a whole, the magi were also believed to have the ability to interpret signs, especially in dreams. Throughout the East, dreams were valued as a means of discerning the future. Even many highly educated Greeks took dream divination seriously, with fourth century BC Greek philosopher Aristotle writing: "We cannot lightly either dismiss it with contempt or give it implicit confidence." Aristotle felt that coincidence could explain most cases where a dream seemed to predict an occurrence, and he certainly didn't believe that dreams were sent by God to guide us. Yet he reserved an admiration for rare individuals who could successfully predict the future via dreams. "Anyone may interpret dreams which are vivid and plain," he said. "The most skillful interpreter of dreams is he who has the faculty of observing resemblances."[5]

By "resemblances," Aristotle meant signs that mirrored reality in the life of the subject. In other words, the best dream diviners were those who knew their clients well and were able to connect an abstract dream to the circumstances of the dreamer. The most successful dream diviners were aware of the fears, preoccupations, and desires of their clients and pandered to them, thus ensuring their own continued favor and employment.

The magi told Astyages, "Your dream, sire, signifies that the offspring of your daughter will reign over Asia instead of you."[6]

Terrified by this prospect, Astyages decided to act on the dream's warning. His daughter Mandana had reached marrying age, which in ancient times came once a girl entered her teens. Determined not to marry her to a Median noble, which could make her offspring eligible for the Median throne, Astyages decided to marry Mandana to a foreigner, a Persian noble. This noble was Cambyses, son of Cyrus I, ruler of the city of Anshan in Persis, a mountainous territory southwest of Ecbatana that had been in time past the first foreign nation to be conquered by the Medes and made a subservient province.

According to Greek historian Herodotus, Cambyses came from a good family, being a descendant of Achaemenes, founder of the Achaemenid clan of Persis' Pasargadae tribe, which provided Persis' ruling class. Just the same, Astyages looked down on the Persian as "much inferior to a Mede of even middle rank."[7] Confident that no Persian could ever rule the Median Empire, Astyages congratulated himself on thwarting his dream by marrying Mandana outside the Median royal house.

Plus, Cambyses possessed what Herodotus described as "a quiet temper," making him seemingly a man who should pose no threat to his father-in-law. Astyages summoned Cambyses to Ecbatana, where the Persian was married to Mandana. Cambyses then took his young bride back to Anshan, the modern Tall-i Malyan, which lies north of Shiraz on a rocky plain in the Zagros Mountains of southwest Iran.

Within a matter of months, three significant events occurred. Old Cyrus I died, Cambyses succeeded him as King of Anshan, and Mandana became pregnant to Cambyses. Soon Mandana's father, Astyages, had another dream about his daughter, now the queen of Anshan. This time, a vine grew from Mandana's womb and encompassed all of Asia Minor. Panicking, Astyages once again summoned the leading magi, who declared that their prince's latest dream once again foreshadowed the reign over Asia by a child of Mandana—in Astyages's stead.

One brutal but simple solution to the problem would have been to kill Mandana, but Astyages apparently cared too much for his daughter to do that. But he didn't care enough for her to spare her child. So, he had Mandana brought to Ecbatana. When she arrived, with her pregnancy well advanced, she was lodged in the royal palace under close guard. It was Astyages's intention to have the child killed once it entered the world.

A boy was duly born—a boy who would ultimately be named after his paternal grandfather Cyrus, pronounced "Kourosh" in Old Persian. Cyrus is the Latinized version of the Greek Cyros, which was how ancient Greek historians wrote Kourosh.

Astyages now summoned the most senior and most loyal Median on his personal staff, a nephew or cousin by the name of Harpagus. It was Harpagus, who was probably in his twenties, to whom Astyages entrusted all his most important chores. Harpagus found Astyages frantic with anxiety. After warning Harpagus not to let him down, the prince issued a chilling order.

"Take the child of my daughter Mandana. Carry him to your home territory. Then kill him there. Bury him as you like."

Harpagus was shocked by this callous command. "Oh, my lord," he replied, as the ramifications of the order sunk in, "I've never let you down in the past, and be assured that in the future I'll take care to never defy your will. If this is what you want, it's up to me to get it done as diligently as possible."[8]

But Harpagus was deeply troubled by the command, which he considered insane. He himself had a three-year-old son and couldn't imagine bringing himself to murder an innocent child. Besides, Mandana's boy was of the same royal blood as himself; he was his relative. Harpagus reasoned that Mandana might one day be called upon to rule Media because Astyages at that time had no son and heir. If Mandana were to take the throne, Harpagus could imagine her torturing and executing him for killing her baby son.

After the baby was taken from its mother and handed to Harpagus, he went home with the child to his wife. In tears, he explained to her the murderous mission given to him by his master, the prince.

"What does your heart tell you to do?" his wife asked, no doubt cradling the infant.

"Not what Astyages wants me to do," Harpagus emotionally replied. "No, he may become even crazier and more frantic than he is now, but I won't be the man to carry out his wish, or even lend a hand to a murder like this." Nonetheless he knew that in taking such a stand, he was endangering himself in the short term. "For my own safety, the child must die," Harpagus finally conceded to his wife after much soul searching. "But someone in Astyages's service other than me must do it."[9]

Harpagus sent for a royal slave, a Persian cattle manager in the king's service by the name of Mithradates. He lived in a village in a mountainous, heavily forested part of Media to the north of Ecbatana, near the Black Sea, and was married to a woman named Cyno who had previously served as a maid at the royal palace. While he was waiting for Mithradates to arrive, Harpagus must have surreptitiously employed the services of a wet nurse to feed the child and keep him alive.

It was a worried Mithradates who set off for the capital. Harpagus had never sent for him before, and this particularly concerned his wife, Cyno. What was more, Cyno was herself pregnant and due to give birth any day, and Mithradates was not happy to leave her. When he reached Ecbatana and was admitted to his master's house in the royal compound, he was astonished to see all the female servants in tears.

"It quite frightened me," he would later tell his wife, "but I went in. The moment I stepped inside, what should I see but a baby lying on the floor, panting and whimpering, and all covered with gold, and wrapped in clothes of such beautiful colors."

Harpagus was there, consoling his wife, for she and the servants knew why Mithradates had been summoned, even though Mithradates himself was still oblivious to the purpose of his visit. As soon as Harpagus saw the herdsman, he ordered him, "Pick up the child, and take him away."[10]

When an astonished Mithradates asked what he was to do with the baby, Harpagus said he was to leave him in the mountains to die, adding that this was Astyages's wish. But he didn't inform Mithradates of the identities of the child's parents. He stressed that if Mithradates failed to carry out the order to kill the baby, he would suffer a slow death at the hands of royal executioners.

Historian Herodotus, who relates this part of the story, says that Harpagus provided Mithradates with a cradle for the child on the journey north, and a servant—probably one of his eunuch bodyguards—to guide him from the city, past the prying eyes of sentries and officials. You would expect that he would also have sent the wet nurse along, to feed and care for the baby on the long journey.

Mithradates, probably driving a donkey cart with the baby and wet nurse in the back, was racking his mind about whose child it could be. "I thought it might be the son of one of the household slaves," he later told his wife. "I did wonder, certainly, to see the gold and the beautiful baby clothes. And I couldn't think why there was such a weeping in Harpagus's house. Well, very soon, as I came away, I got at the truth."

The servant of Harpagus accompanying him conspiratorially shared the names of the boy's parents with him and confirmed that it was Astyages's shocking command that his own grandson be murdered. When Mithradates walked in the door to his home after a journey of some days, he had a bundle in his arms. His wife, Cyno, pale and fearful, demanded to know why Harpagus had summoned him in such a hurry.

"Wife, when I got to the city, I saw and heard such things as I wish to heaven I had never seen," the simple countryman exclaimed, before going on to tell Cyno of how Harpagus had ordered him to take the child away. "And what was I to do with him, do you think? Why, to lay him in the mountains, where the wild beasts are most plentiful." After revealing that Mandana and Cambyses were the boy's parents, he took the baby to his wife and pulled back its swaddling clothes, saying, "And look, here the child is."

At this, Cyno burst into tears. "How fine a child!" she cried. "How beautiful he is!" Clasping her husband's knees, she implored him not to leave the baby in the wild to die.

"But, it's impossible for me to do otherwise," Mithradates replied, declaring that Harpagus would surely send men to check that he had carried out the murder, and a horrible death would be his once they discovered that he had disobeyed Harpagus.[11]

Now Cyno revealed that her tears were not only for the baby in her husband's arms. While Mithradates had been away, Cyno had given birth to a boy. But that boy had been stillborn, and Cyno had been awaiting Mithradates's return so that he could carry out their son's funeral rites. With her personal tragedy about to be compounded by the equally tragic murder of a child, Cyno urged her husband to lay their dead boy in the hills in the place of Mandana's son, after which they could raise the royal baby as their own.

Mithradates thought this an admirable solution. There would be an element of risk involved, but as long as their secret remained with just Cyno and himself, no one else would be the wiser. And they would have a son to raise. Giving the child who would grow to become Cyrus II to his wife to care for—she would have been lactating as a result of her own pregnancy so would be able to feed the boy—Mithradates wrapped the body of his own stillborn son in the clothes of the royal infant and took it to the hills. There, as he sadly watched over it, his baby's body lay exposed for three days.

Then, leaving one of his assistants to watch over the corpse, Mithradates hastened back to Ecbatana, where he reported to Harpagus that the dirty deed had been done and the son of Mandana was dead. Harpagus sent Mithradates home, accompanied by several of the most trustworthy eunuchs of his personal guard. After those bodyguards reported back that they had seen the now decomposing body of a child in the same clothes that had swathed Mandana's son, Harpagus sent Mithradates permission to give the child a fitting funeral. As far as Harpagus was concerned, the matter was now literally dead and buried.

At the palace, Mandana was informed that her son had died from natural causes. Once she had recovered from the birth, no doubt grief stricken, she made her way home to Anshan in Persis, to give her husband, Cambyses, the grim news about the loss of their child. Meanwhile, in the mountains, Mithradates and Cyno set about raising the child of Mandana and Cambyses as their own. Giving the boy the name of Agradates, they agreed to never reveal to him that he wasn't their blood child, let alone tell him that his parents were actually a king and queen.

2

DEPORTING THE JEWS TO BABYLON

THREE YEARS AFTER THE BIRTH OF CYRUS, in 597 BC, the city of Jerusalem fell to invaders following a siege of several months. In the hills of the small kingdom of Judah, which bordered the western side of the Dead Sea, Jerusalem was conquered by the Babylonian army of King Nebuchadnezzar II.[12]

Up until 605 BC, the kingdom of Judah had for some years been controlled by Egypt, but that year, Nebuchadnezzar had defeated the Egyptians in battle and incorporated Judah into his empire. His new conquests stretched from the most easterly branch of the Nile to the Euphrates. The then Jewish king of Judah, Jehoiakim, had been forced to send members of his royal family and other leading Jewish men to Babylon as hostages to peace. Jehoiakim subsequently paid annual tribute of silver and gold to Nebuchadnezzar, as he had previously paid the Pharaoh of Egypt.

This arrangement had lasted four years, until Jehoiakim, a debauched, irreligious ruler who was reputedly covered with tattoos, switched sides, choosing to ally Judah with Egypt and ceasing to pay tribute to Babylon. Nebuchadnezzar had taken his time reacting, methodically recruiting and equipping an army for a fresh campaign against Egypt and the Jews. Built around a core of Babylonian troops, or Chaldeans as the Jews called them, Nebuchadnezzar's army included men conscripted from Syria and other lands in his empire—Moabites and Ammonites, traditionally considered descendants of scriptural figure Lot, nephew of Abraham. Those Babylonian-conquered kingdoms lay east of the Dead Sea in what today is Jordan.

It was only in the last weeks of 598 BC that Nebuchadnezzar crossed the Euphrates and marched into Syria on his campaign to retake Judah. He was soon laying siege to Jerusalem, catching the Jews unprepared for a winter war. When, on March 16, 597 BC, Jerusalem was taken, Nebuchadnezzar captured and executed King Jehoiakim and his senior Jewish commanders. Such was Nebuchadnezzar's disgust at Jehoiakim's duplicity that he had his body tossed beyond the city gates and left to rot.

Nebuchadnezzar installed Jehoiakim's son Jeconiah, also called Jehoiachin, as vassal king of the reconquered Judah, but within three months, the Babylonian king came to suspect Jeconiah of disloyalty and deposed him, replacing him with Jeconiah's younger brother Zedekiah. This time, Nebuchadnezzar sent Jeconiah, his five sons, and members of his royal family, plus numerous other leaders of the Jewish population, to Babylonia for permanent resettlement—the biblical book of Kings puts the number of exiles at 4,600.

Along with captives from other nations, these Jews were herded away, marched east, and settled in colonies across Babylonia—at Babylon itself and in and around other cities including Susa. This was prompted by the fact that the Assyrians, when they'd conquered Babylonia, had severely depopulated the area. Jeconiah remained a political prisoner, but contrary to popular belief, the other Jewish captives were not made slaves in Babylonia, the territory controlled by Babylon, which included a number of other cities. The Jews were given land, permitted to work at their normal occupations—other than as priests of Yahweh, God of the Jews—and paid taxes, enhancing the Babylonian economy. Some would become affluent and accumulate slaves. As for Jeconiah, in 559 BC he would be released at Babylon after thirty-seven years as a close prisoner. Joining the court of the then Babylonian king Amel-Marduk, he would die in the city of Babylon.

However, the captive Jews were not permitted to actively follow their own faith. According to the book of Isaiah, they were required to "bow down to Bel and Nebo." In Mesopotamian culture, Bel was the principal god, equating with the Greek god Zeus and the Romans' Jupiter, or Jove. Bel was a general term meaning both "the Lord of the gods" and "the Lord of the heavens." In Babylon, this supreme god was Marduk. The son of Marduk was Nabu—written as Nebo in the Old Testament. He was an equivalent of both the Greco-Roman god Apollo, son of Zeus/Jupiter, and Mercury, messenger of the gods. In Mesopotamia, Nabu was the god of wisdom and learning and was considered the creator of writing. Many members of Babylonian royalty had Nabu's name incorporated into their own name. Nebuchadnezzar's name, for example, given to him by his father Nabopolassar, meant "Oh, god Nabu, protect my firstborn son."

Some Jewish captives were drafted into the Babylonian army, others into the construction corps, while the most handsome and intelligent young Jewish men were given Babylonian names and selected for training in the Akkadian language of the Babylonians and in Babylonian culture. Some of these young Jews were even recruited into the ranks of the trusted eunuchs in royal service at Nebuchadnezzar's palace, the men who were in closest contact with the monarch on a daily basis. According to biblical tradition, among these Jews chosen for Babylonian re-education were four youths: childhood friends Daniel, Hananiah, Mishael, and

Azariah. They were given the Akkadian names of Belteshazzar, Shadrach, Meshach, and Abednego, all of which related to the Babylonian gods. More about this quartet later.

3

THE BOY IN THE BASKET

SEVEN YEARS AFTER Nebuchadnezzar's conquest of Jerusalem, Cyrus, who then went by the name of Agradates and believed himself to be the son of slaves, celebrated his tenth birthday in the mountains of northern Media. In the year 590 BC, an event occurred that significantly changed Cyrus's life yet again.

The boy's home village adjoined stone night shelters for cattle, called cattle folds, which protected the royal herds in the depths of winter. Many of the men in the village would have—like Cyrus's foster father, Mithradates—been slaves employed as royal cattle herders. They fed the cattle in the folds in winter and herded them up to the mountain pastures in the spring, driving them back in the fall.

One day, ten-year-old Cyrus was playing a game with his fellow children in the village. In this game, the other boys elected him their "king" for the day. The rules of this game of kings allowed Cyrus to appoint his companions to positions in his "court," reflecting those in the royal court at Ecbatana. Some he appointed his doorkeepers, others, his bodyguards, and one, King's Messenger. Others still he ordered to build him a house—like a children's playhouse today, no doubt. But one boy refused to take orders from Cyrus. This was the son of Artembares, who, according to Herodotus, was "a Mede of distinction," a leading noble and member of the royal court. Later events suggest that Artembares held the prestigious post of Cup Bearer to Astyages; if not then, certainly later. His son, on a visit to the village from Ecbatana and one of the boys playing the game of kings, haughtily declared that he wasn't going to take orders from the son of a cowherd—even though he'd joined the others in voting Cyrus king. So Cyrus ordered his "guards" to arrest this boy. For his disobedience, Cyrus then proceeded to give the boy a lashing about the shoulders with a stock whip.

Predictably, on his return to Ecbatana, the boy went crying to his father about his treatment. Artembares was furious, but because Cyrus's foster father, Mithradates, was in the direct employ of the king, he couldn't personally punish Cyrus. Considering his entire family slighted, and determined not to let the matter rest, Artembares sought an audience with the sovereign, taking his son with him.

At this time, King Cyaxares was away on campaign. Over the past year, Cyaxares had been leading the Median army in a war against western neighbors the Lydians, whose empire occupied much of today's western and northern Turkey. Like so many wars, the Media-Lydia conflict had been sparked by a minor disagreement, in this case stemming from an earlier war. Back then, Cyaxares had defeated Scythian invaders from today's southern Siberia. Some surviving Scythians, famously the East's finest archers on foot and horseback, had been permitted to settle in Media in a peace deal agreed with Cyaxares. In return, they were required to give some of the wild beasts caught in their annual hunt to the Median king and allow sons of Median nobles to spend time among them learning Scythian archery skills.

A year or so back, the Scythians had angered King Cyaxares by failing to deliver anything from their hunt. After he took disciplinary measures against them, the Scythians had secretly killed and cooked one of the sons of the Median nobles then living with them and invited the king to a meal of baked boy, which he unwittingly ate. Only after these Scythians subsequently fled northwest to neighboring Lydia had Cyaxares learned the truth. Not unsurprisingly, Cyaxares had exploded with rage. When he demanded the handover of the Scythians, the king of Lydia had refused. So Cyaxares had taken Media to war with Lydia. It was a war that would last for six years.

While Cyaxares was away on campaign, the king's son and heir, Astyages, was left in charge at Ecbatana. So when Artembares came to lodge his complaint against young Cyrus, it was Astyages who sat on the throne to hear him. Artembares, pointing to welts on his son's shoulders resulting from the beating delivered by Cyrus, denounced his son's youthful assailant, declaring, "This, oh prince, is how your slave, the son of a cowherd, heaped insult upon us."[13]

Astyages sent for both Mithradates and young Cyrus to present themselves before him on another day. When they arrived in Ecbatana and were ushered into the royal audience chamber to prostrate themselves before the prince, they found Artembares already present and prostrated before Astyages.

The prince addressed Cyrus directly. "Did you, the son of so lowly a fellow as that..."—he nodded toward Mithradates—"... dare to behave so rudely to the son of this noble, one of the first men of my court?"

"My lord," ten-year-old Cyrus began in his defense, "I only treated him as he deserved. I was chosen king in a game by the boys of our village, because they thought I was the best for the role. He himself was one of the boys who chose me. All the others followed my orders, but he refused, and made fun of them, until at last he got his due reward. If I deserve to suffer punishment for this, here I am, ready to submit to it."[14]

Astyages was shocked by the boy's mature and noble response. And he was struck by a thought. Not only was this boy from the mountains different from other slave boys, but Astyages fancied that he had similar facial features to himself. And his age seemed to tally with that of his grandson, the son of his daughter Mandana, whom he had consigned to death—the boy that Harpagus had assured him had died from exposure in the very mountains that this supposed son of Mithradates hailed from. For a long time, Astyages was silent, deep in thought. Deciding to question Mithradates in private, Astyages turned to his offended noble.

"I promise you, Artembares, that I will settle this business in a way that neither you nor your son will have reason to complain." He then dismissed Artembares from his presence and had his staff take young Cyrus into an inner room, leaving his foster father, Mithradates, on his face before his master. "Where did you get the boy?" Astyages demanded. "Who gave him to you?"

"My lord," Mithradates fearfully replied, "the lad is my own child, begat by myself. The mother who bore him is still alive and lives with me in my house."

But Astyages was buying none of it. "You're very ill-advised to get yourself into such trouble," he growled, nodding to spearmen of his bodyguard, who moved forward and seized Mithradates by the arms. The prince ordered him taken to the rack, for the truth to be tortured from him.

"No, wait!" Mithradates cried as he was being dragged away. He proceeded to tell Astyages the truth about Cyrus, from the first to the last, without concealing a thing, and begged and beseeched his master's forgiveness.

Astyages immediately sent guards to locate Harpagus. When Harpagus arrived, he saw Mithradates in custody in the audience chamber and immediately, fearfully, guessed what was going on.

"By what manner of execution was it, Harpagus," Astyages

asked, calmly and coolly, "that you killed the child of my daughter that I handed over to you?"

Harpagus, realizing the game was up, made no attempt to lie. "Sire, when you gave the child into my hands, I instantly debated with myself how I could go about executing your wishes, and yet, without being unfaithful to you, avoid staining my hands with blood, which, in truth, was your daughter's blood and your own blood." He went on to explain how he had ordered Mithradates to expose the baby in the mountains until it was dead and how he had also sent his most trusted eunuchs to confirm that all had been done as he commanded and view the corpse.

Astyages nodded, then said—without any sign of anger and sounding philosophical about the turn of events—"So, the boy is alive. And things are best as they are. For, the child's fate was a great sorrow to me, and the grief of my daughter touched my heart. Truly, fortune has done us a good turn in this. Go home, then, and send your son to provide company for the newcomer. And tonight, as I mean to sacrifice offerings of thanks for the child's safety to the gods to whom such honor is due, I want you to be a guest at the banquet."

Relieved and overjoyed, Harpagus went home to share with his wife the tidings that instead of being punished for allowing the son of Mandana to live, not only was he being invited to a thanksgiving banquet with the prince, their son was being honored by being made companion to Astyages's newfound grandson. As soon as Harpagus arrived home, he sent for his now thirteen-year-old son, his only child, and instructed the boy to hurry to the royal palace and do whatever Astyages commanded. Away went the excited youth, and Harpagus sought out his wife with the news.

That evening, Harpagus duly attended a feast at the palace, reclining at a table with Astyages and seven other guests, although not in a place of honor on the same couch as Astyages. When Harpagus seemed to have eaten his fill, Astyages called to him,

"How did you enjoy your meal, Harpagus?"

"I enjoyed it immensely, sire," Harpagus replied.

Evidently pleased, Astyages motioned for servants to bring a covered wicker basket and place it before Harpagus. "Open the basket, Harpagus," said Astyages. "Take from it whatever you please."

Thanking the prince, Harpagus lifted the lid of the basket, then froze. Inside the basket were the head, hands and feet of his teenage son. As soon as the boy had arrived at the palace, Astyages had ordered him taken away, executed, then dismembered and cooked. This order was no doubt inspired by the similar cruel act that had ignited the Median-Lydian war. Some parts of the body of Harpagus's son had been roasted, some boiled. These cuts had all been delivered to Harpagus, and while other guests had eaten beef and goat, he had unwittingly eaten the flesh of his son.

"Do you know what beast's flesh you have been eating, Harpagus?" Astyages asked, no doubt with a wicked leer.

Harpagus, very quickly overcoming his revulsion and recovering his equilibrium, put the lid back on the basket and replied, "I know very well. But whatever you do, sire, is agreeable to me."

He subsequently took his son's remains home, to consign them to a funeral pyre. Harpagus never had any more children. Showing no public signs of grief, he gave Astyages the impression that he had learned a bitter lesson and would never disobey him again. As a result, Astyages retained Harpagus as one of his courtiers.

As for Mithradates the cowherd, according to Herodotus, Astyages "was very little further concerned about him." That could be interpreted to mean that he let Mithradates go unpunished. But that is surprising, considering the fact that it was Mithradates who'd made the decision to deceive him and raise Mandana's boy as his own. And would Astyages really let him off after delivering such a vile punishment to Harpagus? In fact, Herodotus's comment could be read to mean that Astyages wiped his hands of Mithradates, dismissing him from his service and banning him from gainful employment. In that way, Astyages would never have to be concerned about him again.

This fate seems to be confirmed by other ancient authors, Ctesias and Nicolaus, who said that Cyrus's foster father turned to banditry—his only recourse if he'd lost his job and was an official outcast. The fate of bandits was and is rarely a pleasant one, and Mithradates was probably caught and executed within a few years. Ctesias and Nicolaus seem to give weight to that possibility by adding that Mithradates's wife, Cyrus's foster mother, became a goatherd, perhaps in her widowhood. Certainly by the time that Cyrus came to power and was in a position to help them, there was no mention of his foster parents. They had almost certainly both died by then.

There only remained the question of what Astyages was going to do with young Cyrus.

4

SAVED BY THE MAGI

CONTRARY TO WHAT ASTYAGES had led Harpagus to believe, the prince had not yet decided to embrace Cyrus as his long-lost grandson. To guide his decision on the boy's fate, Astyages sent for the same magi who, years earlier, had interpreted his dreams about the water and vine emanating from his daughter.

Astyages began by asking the magi to revisit their interpretation of his two dreams all those years before. They replied that, if the boy still lived, the dreams indeed prophesied that he would one day become a king. In response to this, Astyages informed them that the boy was very much alive. Then he told them all about the boys' game in the mountain village, where Cyrus had been made a king.

"Tell me," he then glumly asked, "what do you think this all means?"

"If the boy survives," said the spokesman of the magi after they had consulted, "and has ruled as a king without any tricks or connivance, then in that case, we urge you to cheer up and not worry about him anymore. He won't reign a second time. For we've found that even oracles can sometimes be fulfilled in an unimportant way. And dreams, still more frequently, have amazingly simple outcomes."

"That's what I was inclined to think," said Astyages with relief. "The boy having already been king, the dream has been realized, and I have nothing more to fear from him." But almost as soon as he'd said this, his confidence in the apparent meaning of the dream waned, and he began to doubt the motives of the magi. "Be careful to counsel me the best you can for the safety of my house, and your own best interests," he cautioned them.

The magi, although appreciating the threat to themselves, stuck by their view that the dreams had been realized, reminding Astyages that if they were wrong and the boy did one day become king, being a Persian, he would take away the freedom of the Medes, in which case, they, the Median magi, would lose their honored position and share of government.

"We therefore have every reason to forecast accurately for you and your rule," the magi concluded. "Be assured, if we saw any reason for present fear, we wouldn't keep it back from you. But, truly, we are persuaded that the dream has been realized in this harmless way. And so, with our fears abated, we recommend that you banish yours. As for the boy, we recommend that you send him away to Persis, to his father and mother."

This response made sense to Astyages and pleased him. Dismissing the magi with his thanks, he sent for young Cyrus.

"My child," he said to the boy, "I was led to do you a wrong by a dream which has come to nothing. From that wrong you were saved by your own good fortune. Go now with a light heart to Persis. I will provide you with an escort. Go, and when you reach your journey's end, you will see your father and mother—quite different people from Mithradates the cowherd and his wife."[15]

This totally mystified Cyrus, who had no idea of his true family background. But once he was on his way to Persis from Ecbatana, clad in princely clothes and escorted by troops of the royal guard, the commander of his escort solved the mystery for him by telling him who his real parents and grandparents were. His arrival at Anshan, the Persian capital, was totally unheralded, and now his mother and father were in for a shock, as the son they had thought dead for ten years walked in the door.

Many a tear would have been shed by Mandana and Cambyses as they reunited with their boy, and he told them about how he'd been raised by Cyno and Mithradates. But before long, the youth's stories about what a loving mother Cyno had been, and his tears for her, began to grate with his natural parents. He "filled his whole talk with her praises," says Herodotus. "It was always Cyno—Cyno was everything." To put a stop to this reverence for a cowherd's wife, Mandana and Cambyses, "catching the word at his mouth," as Herodotus puts it, apparently forbade Cyrus to ever utter Cyno's name again.

In her jealousy of Cyrus's affection for Cyno, Mandana, it seems, declared that Cyno was nothing but a bitch. And this gave rise to a famous folk tale. Herodotus says that Mandana and Cambyses contrived a legend to explain away Cyno and explain the boy's miraculous survival when consigned to the wilds to die—"to persuade Persians that there was a special providence in his preservation," says Herodotus.

Central to this myth was the fact that Mithradates the cowherd was named for the principal Persian god, Mithra. According to Persian mythology, Mithra had slain a bull while watched by the sun god and the moon goddess, the next most important Persian deities. Also observing the slaying of the bull were four beasts sacred to the gods: a snake, a scorpion, a raven, and a dog.

According to the Cyrus myth created by his blood parents, which Herodotus says was current in his day, Cyrus, abandoned in the wild, had been suckled by a wild dog until Mithra sent a cowherd to save him. This was designed to show that Cyrus had been chosen to lead his people by God—in this case, by Bel, or the Lord, known as Mithra to the Persians and Marduk to the Babylonians. The Old Persian and Median word for a female dog, or bitch, was *spaka*, and in this mythical version of Cyrus's preservation the name of Mithradates's wife became Spaco, not Cyno.[16]

This myth was very similar to that which surrounded the foundation of Rome, with Romulus and Remus being suckled in the wilds by a wolf. Although Rome had been founded some 150 years prior to the birth of Cyrus, the she-wolf myth about Rome's origins can only be dated back to the third century BC and may have been influenced by Herodotus's earlier account of Cyrus and the Persian Empire's so-called Foundation Myth. Mithraism, the worship of Mithra, would in fact become popular throughout the Roman Empire, especially among slaves and the lower ranks of the army, rivaling Christianity until the latter became the religion of the emperors, after which followers of Mithra were officially persecuted, and Mithraism was stamped out.

So now, Cyrus, instructed to forget his foster parents, was raised by his real parents at Anshan as a prince and heir to his father's throne, yet still a vassal of the Persians' overlords, the Medes.

5

JERUSALEM DESTROYED

JUST A YEAR AFTER CYRUS WAS SENT to his real parents in Anshan, in 589 BC, a Babylonian army led by King Nebuchadnezzar II once again marched into the kingdom of Judah and laid siege to its capital, Jerusalem. Once again, the Jews had turned against their Babylonian overlords, with young King Zedekiah allying against Nebuchadnezzar with Pharaoh Apries of Egypt—called Hophra in the Old Testament.

The Jews had been prepared for this siege and held out for much longer than they previously had done after the Babylonian army surrounded Jerusalem. Scholars believe that the Jewish defenders withstood the siege for between eighteen and thirty months. But, as in the past, and as would be the case in the future, Jerusalem fell to the attackers. It was hunger that finally defeated them; defenders even resorted to cannibalism to survive.

But when Nebuchadnezzar entered the captured city, he discovered that King Zedekiah, his family, and senior members of the court had escaped. The Jewish king wasn't on the run for long. He and his party fled north, only to be recognized while they were crossing the plains of Jericho and taken prisoner. Once Zedekiah and his family were brought before Nebuchadnezzar, they found that the Babylonian monarch had lost any patience he'd had with his rebellious Jewish subjects. Zedekiah was made to watch as his young sons were executed before his eyes—and then his eyes were gouged out. In chains, the blinded king was sent to Babylon with his remaining family and courtiers. He would die there a prisoner.

Nebuchadnezzar appointed a Jew by the name of Gedaliah as governor of the Babylonian province of Yehud Medinata, which included the former kingdom of Judah. Governor Gedaliah was installed at the town of Mizpah, ten miles north of Jerusalem, along with family members, eunuch servants, and a small guard of Babylonian troops. As Nebuchadnezzar departed Jerusalem, he instructed the commander of his royal guard, Nebuzarradan, to loot and utterly destroy the city.

The Babylonian destruction of Jerusalem was total. Over weeks of demolition, the city's walls were torn down. The buildings within the walls were torched and torn apart brick by clay brick. The ninth century BC Temple of Solomon was burned, with all that remained then pulled down. "Zion is a wilderness, Jerusalem a desolation," says the book of Isaiah. "Our holy and our beautiful house [the Temple], where our fathers praised you, is burned up with fire, and all our pleasant things are laid waste." All the gold and silver offerings filling the Temple and the sacred religious artifacts of the Temple were removed to Babylon, to be stored in royal treasuries along with the loot from other foreign cities captured in Nebuchadnezzar's campaigns.

Governor Gedaliah encouraged the return of many Jews who'd fled east of the Dead Sea to escape Nebuchadnezzar, urging them to harvest the grapes and other fruits in the region's deserted farmlands and settle at Mizpah. Among the hundreds who returned were eleven men bent on assassinating Gedaliah. Pretending friendship, they met with Gedaliah just two months after his appointment by Nebuchadnezzar, produced weapons, and wiped out his guard, then murdered Gedaliah and all his family except his daughters.

As the chief assassin went on a killing spree, filling a pit with Jewish victims, surviving Jews deserted him for a new leader. As the assassin fled east, the remaining Jews, fearing the vengeful return of Nebuchadnezzar's troops, abandoned Mizpah and trekked south to find sanctuary in Egypt. A deathly silence fell over the site of Jerusalem. Ever since it had been seized from its Canaanite owners by a Jewish army under King David, the City of Peace had attracted conquerors like bears to honey. Now a blackened, uninhabited ruin, it was to lay neglected, although not forgotten, for decades, until the rise of Cyrus.

6

IN THE COURT
OF THE KING

Two years after the destruction of Jerusalem by the Babylonians, peace came to the Middle East with the end of the war between Media and Lydia. For six years, the Medes and the Lydians had been slugging it out without one side gaining the upper hand. Sometimes the Medians won a battle; sometimes the Lydians won. There had even been an indecisive nighttime battle. At the end of each year, the two armies had marched home to spend the winter licking wounds, training new recruits, and amassing new stocks of weapons and supplies. Each spring, they marched back to resume hostilities where they'd left off.

In the spring of 585 BC, the two armies faced off beside the Halys River, today's Kizilirmak River in Turkey. It was in the last days of May that the armies of King Cyaxares of Media and King Alyattes of Lydia formed up to do battle, each placing the river on one flank to avoid being outflanked on that side, as was the custom. As May 28 dawned, the battle preliminaries commenced.

According to Herodotus, as the day began to heat up, the moon slid in front of the sun, turning day into night.

As we now know, this was a lunar eclipse, but the troops on either side had no knowledge of the natural motions of the moon around the earth, and even though noted astronomer Thales of Miletus had predicted this very event, the rank and file felt sure this eclipse was an act of the gods. Terrified, they refused to fight. The two kings sent each other emissaries, and the short-lived Battle of Halys, to be dubbed the Battle of the Eclipse by later historians, was terminated, as was the Median-Lydian war, with a peace treaty.

That treaty marked the Halys as the border between Media and Lydia from that day forward. Plus, to cement the peace and create an alliance between their two powerful nations, the Lydian king promised his daughter Aryenis in marriage to King Cyaxares's son Astyages—whose first wife, the Armenian princess Tigranuhi, was the mother of Mandana and grandmother of Cyrus. This meant that Media now had alliances bound by marriage with both Lydia and Babylon—Astyages's sister Amytis was married to King Nebuchadnezzar.

The Lydian-Median treaty was sealed by a blood oath, in which the two kings created slight wounds on their arms and then each sucked out and swallowed a mouthful of the other's blood. Not many months after Astyages was promised Aryenis as a wife, his father, the hard-soldiering Cyaxares, died in his bed. Now, after a wait of many years, Astyages was King of Media. And as Astyages's life changed, so, too, did that of young Cyrus of Persis.

We are told by both Xenophon and Nicolaus that when Cyrus was in his teens, his mother took him to Ecbatana to see his grandfather King Astyages. Xenophon put Cyrus's age at twelve or a little older at the time. Nicolaus says Cyrus was fifteen, and this tallies with the year that Astyages became king and suggests that the Ecbatana visit by Mandana and Cyrus was for Astyages's 585 BC coronation, an event which Mandana, as Astyages's eldest daughter and heir, would have been required to attend, as would the king's grandson. We aren't told whether Cyrus's father, Cambyses, was also in attendance, but as a vassal king subject to Astyages's commands, it's probable that he was.

By this time, Astyages wore a full, dark, curled beard in the fashion of the era, and, as Xenophon describes him, was adorned in extravagant purple robes and tunics, jangled with golden necklaces and bracelets, and was trying to defy signs of aging by wearing a wig of dark ringlets—he was probably bald underneath. His eyes were circled with dark eyeliner, his cheeks painted red.[17]

The new king was impressed by the now fifteen-year-old Cyrus, and probably a little threatened. According to Nicolaus, Cyrus had spent part of his youth in the tribal territory of his father's Pasargadae clan in Persis, and it's likely Cyrus had summered with his Pasargadae relatives, improving his riding, hunting, and fighting skills in competition with his cousins. Herodotus says that Cyrus became known as "the bravest and most popular of his peers" as he grew to manhood.

According to both Xenophon and Nicolaus, King Astyages decided to keep Cyrus close to him, retaining him at Ecbatana and sending his mother home to Anshan. Xenophon says that Astyages treated Cyrus royally, having him trained to ride, giving him Mede horses, and taking him on royal hunts. Yet other more reliable sources contradict Xenophon's claim that Cyrus was treated lovingly by Astyages, instead portraying Astyages as a cruel and paranoid grandfather.

Ctesias and Nicolaus offer a very different and more credible account of Cyrus's time at his grandfather's court. They say that King Astyages appointed Cyrus to his household staff, working in the bowels of the royal palace, where Astyages's eunuchs could keep an eye on him. Cyrus, they say, started out working for the palace's chief decorator before being transferred to the palace treasurer's staff. This treasurer treated Cyrus cruelly, even though the young man was the king's grandson; the fact that Cyrus had a Persian father counted against him.

As the years passed, Cyrus escaped the unpleasant palace treasurer with a transfer to the department of the chief torchbearer. And then one day, the royal Cup Bearer came down with a fever. Modern writers describe an ancient cup bearer as a sort of butler. Xenophon says he attended the king's table to personally ladle out wine from a large bowl into individual goblets—but not before he poured a little into his own cupped hand to sample it and test it for poison. It was both a highly responsible and a potentially dangerous post.

Astyages's Cup Bearer was named Sacas, according to Xenophon, but he could have confused this man with the senior eunuch Petisacas, who later served on Cyrus's staff. According to the more reliable Nicolaus, this official's name was Artembares, and the implication is that this was the very same Artembares who had complained to Astyages about ten-year-old Cyrus whipping his son. With Artembares confined to his bed, King Astyages appointed Cyrus to fill in for him until he recovered.

Via his pleasing personality, Cyrus eventually became such a favorite of the king's that when Artembares subsequently died, Astyages made Cyrus's Cup Bearer role permanent and endowed him with Artembares's estate and numerous other gifts, overlooking the dead man's family, including the son who'd refused to do Cyrus's bidding during their childhood game of kings.

After Cyrus had served as Cup Bearer for some years, Astyages sent him as a royal envoy on a special mission. Astyages had received a message from Onaphernes, ruler of the Cadusii tribe, which inhabited the Elburz Mountains on the southwest coast of the Caspian Sea. The Cadusians had been a troublesome thorn in Media's side for years, raiding Median territory on foot then melting back into the mountains. Unbeknownst to his people, Onaphernes was proposing either a truce or an alliance with Media, and he had asked Astyages to send a trustworthy emissary for secret discussions. Astyages sent Cyrus, giving him forty days to complete his mission.

Ctesias explains that, on this mission, Cyrus met a fellow who was to become his faithful right-hand man. En route to Cadusia, Cyrus encountered a Persian, apparently a horse groom, who had marks of a whipping on his back and horse dung in a basket. This fellow's name was Oebares—also written Oebaras by differing sources. The horse dung in a basket sounds comical, but it was valued as a fertilizer, and in the dried form was burned on fires in lieu of other flammable material. Plus, horses were sacred to Persian nobility and were often sacrificed to Mithra. So, much meaning would later be attributed to Oebares's equine connections.

The two men immediately hit it off, as Cyrus found Oebares bright and perceptive. Inviting Oebares to join him, Cyrus gave him a horse, outfitted him in plush robes, and provided servants from his own household. According to Ctesias, as they continued on the road to Cadusia, Oebares suggested that some bold Persian should ally himself with the Cadusians and, in coordination with them, lead the Persian people in rising against Astyages and throwing off the Median yoke.

"If a man were to appear who did all this," Cyrus is said to have responded as they rode, "would you share the dangers at his side?"

"Yes," Oebares spiritedly returned, "especially if it were you." But, he added, if that man wasn't Cyrus, "I'd do it whoever appeared."[18]

Oebares would loyally serve at Cyrus's side through the adventures that lay ahead. As for the mission to Onaphernes, it seems to have proven a failure. Although the Cadusians are listed among Cyrus's allies in years to come, there is no mention by any source of the Cadusians rising in rebellion in concert with Cyrus, nor of any outcome for Astyages from Cyrus's mission to Onaphernes. In all probability, Cyrus was unable to organize a secret rendezvous with the Cadusian leader and returned to Ecbatana empty-handed. But now, he had Oebares at his side. And as history has shown, every great man needs an equally able lieutenant.

7

LEADING THE PERSIAN
REVOLT

B Y THE SUM M ER OF 552 BC, Cyrus was forty-eight years old
and still working in the palace of King Astyages at Ecbatana.
Astyages had kept a tight rein on his grandson, but in 560 or 559
BC, he had permitted Cyrus to wed. His bride was a Persian girl,
Cassandana—written as Cassandane by Greek authors—daughter
of Pharnaspes, a Persian noble of the Achaemenid clan.

The paranoid Astyages, who had reigned for twenty-six years
and was now well into old age, had no intention of permitting
Cyrus to marry a Mede and produce an heir who could one day
challenge for the Median throne. By all accounts, Cyrus and Cassandana adored each other, even though it would have been an
arranged marriage, with Cassandana brought from Persis for the
wedding.

Cassandana was probably a teenager. She soon became pregnant by her new, older husband, and in 559 BC, she gave birth to a
son, whom Cyrus named Cambyses in honor of his father. While
Cyrus had to remain at the palace in Ecbatana, Cassandana prob-

ably gave birth to the baby back in Anshan, at the palace of Cyrus's parents. The couple seems to have been kept apart for much of the next eight or nine years—their next child wouldn't be born until 550 BC.

Over this period, Astyages's relative Harpagus, who'd failed in his appointed task of murdering Cyrus when he was a baby, fostered Cyrus's friendship, giving him gifts and sending him friendly messages. Although Harpagus had remained in Astyages's favor, he had secretly never forgiven the king for executing his son. As Astyages's rule grew increasingly harsh, Harpagus came to the conclusion that Media needed a new sovereign. Other senior Median nobles Harpagus sounded out felt much the same way, although none were prepared to themselves move against Astyages. They agreed with Harpagus that what they needed was a potential challenger with Median royal blood.

The most obvious choice was one of the two sons of Astyages's youngest daughter, Amytis, sister of Cyrus's morher—not to be confused with Astyages's sister, the queen of Babylon, after whom she had obviously been named. These boys had been. These boys had been fathered by Amytis's Median noble husband, Spitamas, governor of the home province of Media—an appointment Astyages had made as a wedding present. While Amytis's boys had the required royal blood, both were still young and immature, and if Astyages were to die now, their unpopular father, Spitamas, would probably attempt to rule through them. Cyrus, on the other hand, had the blood, the maturity, and the ability to lead.

Harpagus was able to convince leading men at the Median court, including a noble by the name of Mazares, to join him in backing Cyrus if he led the men of Persis in rising against Astyages. As would become apparent, this backing would only be forthcoming if Cyrus actively kept his mother's people, the Medes, on an equal footing with his father's people, the Persians, once he came to power. The Median nobles wanted a share of empire, not a new order where Medes became the slaves of Persians. But how was Harpagus to communicate the conspirators' readiness to support an uprising by Cyrus without raising suspicion?

According to Herodotus, Harpagus took a freshly killed hare, carefully slit open its belly in a way that didn't damage the fur, then inserted a message, presumably written on a long, thin clay tablet, and sewed the incision closed. He then gave the hare to one of his most faithful slaves, disguised him as a hunter, complete with a net that hunters of small game used, and sent him to Cyrus to deliver the secret message.

Herodotus says that Cyrus was then in Persis, but historian Nicolaus and subsequent events tell us that Cyrus was at Ecbatana all this time. Logic also suggests that a hare sent on the long journey from Ecbatana to Anshan would have arrived in less than appetizing condition and would have attracted suspicion. On the other hand, a freshly caught hare taken from Harpagus's house to the royal palace across town in Ecbatana would have arrived in prime condition. And a servant taking a hare into the palace kitchens, where Cyrus worked in his capacity as Cup Bearer, wouldn't have drawn a second glance.

"Paunch the animal yourself," Harpagus's servant whispered to Cyrus as he handed over the hare, "when no one else is present."

Cyrus duly cut open the hare and discovered the message:

> The time has come when you can take your revenge on Astyages.... I don't think you're ignorant of what he did to you, nor of what I suffered at his hands because I gave you to the cowherd and didn't put you to death. Listen to me now, and follow my advice, and all of Astyages's empire will be yours. Raise the standard of revolt in Persis, and then march straight on Media. Whether Astyages appoints me to command his forces against you or whether he appoints another of the Median princes, all will go as you would wish. They will be the first to fall away from him, and joining your side, work to overturn his power. Be assured, we on our part are ready; so, do your part, and quickly![19]

Alerted to the intent of the Median nobles, Cyrus now had to find a way to get to Persis to instigate a revolt among his own people. Only several times in the past twenty-six years had Astyages permitted Cyrus to go home to Anshan to visit his family. According to Ctesias, Cyrus's new assistant Oebares had been quietly urging him to lead the Persians in revolt despite the failure of his plan to recruit Cadusian support. Now that Harpagus and the Median nobles had indicated they were behind him, and with word arriving from Anshan that Cyrus's father, Cambyses, was ill, Oebares suggested that the time was right for Cyrus ask permission for a home visit.

So, Cyrus approached Astyages, telling him that his father was unwell and promising to make sacrifices at his expense in Astyages's name at Anshan if he let him go home. The Medians and the Persians worshipped a similar pantheon of gods, based around seven major gods and hundreds, if not thousands, of minor deities—seven being considered a sacred and powerful number throughout the Middle East. Herodotus tells us that the seven principal gods of the Persians began with Mithra, personification of Jupiter, king of the gods, whom the Greeks called Zeus. The sun and the moon followed in order of importance, with the gods of the earth, fire, water, and the winds making up the pantheon of seven. Both the Persians and Medes referred to their principal deity as Bel.

Astyages may have been flattered by Cyrus's offer to sacrifice in his name, but he wasn't prepared to let him off the leash. He refused to grant Cyrus permission to leave Ecbatana. When Cyrus despondently told Oebares this, Oebares cheered him by suggesting he wait a few days and then try again—only, this time, he said, Cyrus should ask a trusted eunuch on the king's staff to make the request on his behalf.

Taking Oebares's advice, Cyrus approached an influential eunuch. Ancient engravings depict eunuchs as clean-shaven, apparently a mark of their class—a third, artificially sexless class between male and female in the ancient world. The eunuch who agreed to put in a good word for Cyrus is not named. Several days later, at dinner, Cyrus made sure that the king's cup was never empty, and Astyages became merry. As Cyrus was leaving the dining room, he gave the cooperative eunuch a sign, and in his absence, the eunuch made the request on his behalf. Astyages then called for Cyrus to return.

Smiling at his grandson when Cyrus bowed down before him, the wine-soaked king said, "Cyrus, I grant you five months' leave. Be back in the sixth month."[20]

Cyrus appointed a replacement Cup Bearer to fill in for him, and overnight, Oebares made final preparations for the trip south. At the crack of dawn the next morning, before Astyages could awaken and change his mind, Cyrus and Oebares rode out of Ecbatana with their servants and pack animals.

Ctesias claimed that Cyrus then dispatched a message to his father, Cambyses, in distant Anshan, to urgently send 1,500 mounted fighting men and 5,000 foot soldiers to meet him at the Persian city of Hyrba, not far from the border with Media. This isn't credible. If any troops were permanently stationed in Anshan, they would have been Median, and there is no indication that standing military forces of any nationality were present in Persis at this time. Even if Cambyses recruited and equipped 6,500 Persian fighting men locally, it would have taken far longer than the few days that Ctesias says it took for this force to join Cyrus.

According to Herodotus, Cyrus in fact sent written messages to the chiefs of the then three principal tribes of Persis: his father's Pasargadae, the Maraphii, and the Maspii, summoning them to a meeting with him at Hyrba. The seven other tribes of Persia were dependent on these three, says Herodotus, and would follow their lead. In his letters to the three tribes, Cyrus claimed to be acting on the king's behalf, saying that Astyages had made him his general.

In Ecbatana several nights later, Astyages was at dinner and being entertained as usual by concubines from his harem, dancers, and players of the cithara, or zither, a stringed instrument that was an advancement on the simple Greek lyre—we derive the guitar from the cithara, in name and form. According to Ctesias, as Astyages dined and drank, one of his female entertainers sang a song that went:

> Although the lion had the wild boar in his power,
> He let him go into his lair.
> He has become mightier there,
> And will give the lion much grief,
> And despite being weaker,
> Will end up subduing one stronger.[21]

Paranoid Astyages became highly alarmed by the song. To him, Cyrus was the wild boar, and he the lion. Urgently, he summoned the captain of his royal guard, ordering him take three hundred cavalrymen and track down Cyrus and require him to return to Ecbatana.

"And if he doesn't come," Astyages added, "cut off his head and bring him back like that."[22]

The captain immediately set off in pursuit of Cyrus with three hundred well-armed cavalrymen. Late one afternoon, the captain and his cavalry overtook Cyrus's column on the road, not far short of the Median border with Persis and a day's hard ride from the Persian city of Hyrba. When the captain passed on the king's instruction that Cyrus was to return with him, Cyrus smiled.

"If my master summons me," Cyrus said, "why would I hesitate to go?" It being late in the day, he suggested they set off for the return to Ecbatana first thing in the morning. In the meantime, he proposed that the two parties set up camp together for the night while his servants prepared a meal for them all. The captain, no doubt relieved that the king's grandson was being so amenable, agreed.[23]

As tents were erected, Cyrus had a large number of cattle and oxen butchered and roasted in the Persian style. He then produced stocks of the best royal wine that he was carrying in his baggage train and plied the captain and his troops with all the meat they could eat and all the wine they could drink. When the glutted soldiers all fell into a drunken sleep, Cyrus, Oebares, and their men quietly slipped from camp, mounted up, and rode away, heading for Hyrba.

8

CYRUS'S FIRST BATTLE

CYRUS AND HIS LIEUTENANT Oebares reached the Persian city of Hyrba in the early hours of the morning and gained admittance while the population slept. Waking the city governor, Cyrus commanded him to arm every able-bodied man.

When day broke, back on the road to Hyrba, the commander of the three hundred Median cavalry awoke to find that his quarry had disappeared. He roused his men and angrily set off once more in pursuit. When the cavalry reached the outskirts of Hyrba, it was to find all the townsmen waiting for them, many hundreds in number, lined up in battle order outside the city walls, no doubt rudely armed with rough-hewn pikes and farmers' scythes. Commanding the Persians on the right wing was Cyrus, while Oebares commanded on the left wing; only they and a few of their followers were mounted.

The Median riders charged toward Cyrus, bent on killing or capturing him, and a bloody little battle ensued. With their focus on Cyrus, the cavalrymen would have paid the townsmen little attention, and it's likely that Oebares led the Persian left wing in wrapping around behind the Median riders, surrounding them. According to Ctesias, Cyrus and three other Persians did most of the killing. This quartet succeeded in slaying close to two hundred and fifty of the Medians before the surviving cavalrymen broke away and fled back to Media, to report to King Astyages that they had failed in their mission. Thus the short, sharp Battle of Hyrba became the first victory of the Persian war of liberation.[24]

Cyrus, having killed his grandfather's troops and raised the standard of rebellion, knew he could not turn back now. When the chiefs and clan chiefs of the three main Persian tribes joined him at Hyrba, he failed to tell them about the little battle that had taken place outside the city; the bodies of the dead and their horses and equipment would have been collected, the former for hurried cremation, the latter for use by the rebels.

Still claiming to be acting on Astyages's behalf, Cyrus surprised the chieftains by giving them a brief instruction: "I command you to go and bring your men, each with his reaping-hook."[25]

Perplexed, the chieftains went away.

While Cyrus was waiting for these men to return, messengers arrived from King Astyages, bearing a demand from Cyrus's grandfather that he present himself before him at once.

"Tell Astyages that I will appear before him sooner than he will like," Cyrus replied, sending the messengers back to Ecbatana.[26]

Perhaps a week or so after they had been sent away, as commanded, the Persian chieftains returned to Cyrus with thousands of men equipped with scythes. Cyrus then led this host to a tract of land outside the city. Between two and three miles long and about the same in width, it was covered with thorny bushes.

"Clear this before the day is out," Cyrus instructed.[27]

So the men toiled in the heat of the day, and the tract of land was cleared. At the end of the day, Cyrus instructed the men to bathe the following morning and then come to him in the afternoon.

The next day, while his men relaxed, Cyrus had all his father's flocks of sheep and goats in the area collected and slaughtered, and even had his baggage oxen butchered. Wine in store at Hyrba was brought out, and bread of the choicest kinds baked. That afternoon, when the men came to him as instructed, he bade them lie on the grass. His servants and the townspeople then served them a massive feast. When the meal was over and the men were in good spirits, Cyrus addressed them.

"Which did you like best?" he called. "Today's work, or yesterday's?"

This brought a sea of smiles and a gale of comments, and the observation from one of the chiefs, "Cyrus, the contrast is certainly strong. Yesterday brought us only what was bad; today, all that is good."

Nodding, Cyrus said, "Men of Persis, this is exactly how things stand in your lives. If you choose to do what I propose, you can enjoy these and ten thousand similar delights, and never lower yourself to the toil of slaves. But if you don't, prepare yourself for countless days as hard as yesterday. Now, follow my lead, and be free! As for myself, I feel that I am destined by Providence to undertake your liberation. As for you, I know you're not the slightest inferior to the Medes in anything, least of all in bravery." This must have brought cheers. "Revolt, therefore, from Astyages," called Cyrus. "Today!"[28]

The Persians on the field that day rose up to join Cyrus in going to war for their liberty, and the chieftains went away to recruit and arm the men of all the Persian tribes. Although Cyrus's father Cambyses was the king of Anshan, it was Cyrus who now led the Persian people in their revolt against Median rule. Cambyses would join his son at the Median border, but he was now elderly and unwell. Also, we're told that Cambyses was not exactly sold on the idea of rebellion.

In Ecbatana, meanwhile, King Astyages was in a rage. "I resolved often enough not to treat bad men well," Herodotus reports him declaring, "but I've been tricked by fine words all the same."

The first thing he did was summon Harpagus and his other senior nobles, men who were tied to the throne by blood and to whom he would entrust command of his military forces. He himself had little military experience or know-how; that had been his father's domain. Apart from his royal guard, Astyages didn't maintain a standing army. Like his father, he conscripted rural workers and townspeople into his army as and when he needed to go to war. Now, he ordered mass mobilization throughout his empire.

According to Ctesias, a million foot soldiers and 200,000 cavalry were now recruited and equipped across the Median Empire in the face of Cyrus's Persian revolt, and 3,000 chariots built or taken from storage. This mobilization, together with the manufacture of sufficient weapons, ammunition, and armor to equip 1.2 million men, would take close to a year to complete.

In Persis, Cyrus was also preparing for war. He had at last been able to reunite with his wife, Cassandana; in 550 BC, she would give birth to their next child. But his thoughts were occupied with defeating Astyages. Ctesias, who estimated that there were 400,000 adult Persian men at this time, would claim that under King Cambyses's direction 300,000 javelin-equipped Persian foot soldiers, 50,000 cavalrymen, and one hundred chariots would join Cyrus. Even if such numbers of Persian men were armed during the rebellion, modern historians estimate that no more than 50,000 cavalry and infantry were to join Cyrus at the Median border for the commencement of the war proper.

Cyrus was particularly short of cavalry, because there were far fewer horses in the Persian mountains than on the plains of Media. "There were two gifts he would never refuse," says Xenophon, "horses and good weapons." Xenophon, in fact, says that even four years after this, Cyrus's cavalry arm numbered just 10,000 men.

Xenophon meanwhile confirms Ctesias's number of one hundred chariots taking the field for Cyrus at this time, a far cry from the 3,000 that were to equip Astyages's vastly larger army. But, says Xenophon, Cyrus's war machines were no ordinary chariots. The normal chariot of the era went back hundreds of years to Trojan times. The old chariot was a light vehicle pulled by two horses. With low sides, it had a bench seat that ran from side to side, much like a seat in a rowboat. The driver sat on this seat, while behind him stood a noble who would hurl javelins at the enemy, then dismount to fight on foot. Meanwhile his driver kept his chariot close by, waiting to whisk the noble away from trouble if need be.

Hundreds of years later British tribes would still be going to war in a simple version of the Trojan chariot. Their Roman opponents, including Julius Caesar and the legions of the imperial era, never used chariots as war machines. They knew better. Targeting the chariots' unprotected horses with javelin-fire rather than their crews, the Romans devastated the chariot formations of the southern British tribes and the Caledonians of northern Britannia, winning major victories against massive odds. Six hundred years earlier, Cyrus also saw the vulnerability of the traditional chariot and invented a stunning new version.

Cyrus's new war chariot had stronger wheels than usual, to carry a heavier load and to resist the shock of collision, and longer axles to broaden the vehicle's base. "The driver's seat was changed into what might be called a turret," says Xenophon, "stoutly built of timber and reaching up to the elbow, leaving the driver room to manage the horses above the rim." Sharp iron scythes two feet long were attached to the axles on each side, with others inclining earthward from the chariot's base to pierce any man finding himself run over by the vehicle. The sole crewman, the standing driver, was covered entirely with bronze armor and a helmet with just a slit for his eyes. Because the chariot was so heavy, it was drawn by four horses, not two. Centuries later, the Romans would adopt this four-horse chariot design, apart from the scythes, for their racing chariots. But unlike the Roman chariot's horses, the horses pulling Cyrus's war chariots were heavily clad with armor.

Cyrus also altered the chariot's tactical use. Rather than follow the traditional tactics of harassing enemy lines by running parallel to them or diving in and out on hit-and-run raids, Cyrus's chariot corps would drive straight at enemy lines. If enemy troops didn't break in fear and run as these massive chariots charged into them, they would be mown down, with a gap created in their line, which following cavalry or infantry could surge through and exploit. According to Xenophon, the heavy war chariot invented by Cyrus was still in use by the Persian army in his day, a century after Cyrus created it.

Xenophon also says that Cyrus's army would eventually be equipped with several hundred of these maxi chariots. Another two hundred came from allies or were refitted and upgraded old-style chariots captured from the Medians. The first batch of one hundred would require considerable resources and craftsmen and the training of 400 powerful horses. Xenophon claimed that one of Cyrus's commanders even had an eight-horse chariot built for himself, a massively wide vehicle involving two yokes—a vehicle that invariably must have proven difficult to handle on rough ground.

Over the winter months of 551-550 BC, the Persians labored feverishly to create Cyrus's new chariot arm and to equip and train recruits to face the Median attack, which they knew must come in the spring. According to Xenophon, Cyrus was meticulous in how he organized his small army, dividing it into regiments of 10,000 men, each led by a noble. Every regiment, he says, was divided into a company of 420 men, led by a captain. And each company was divided into seventy squads of six men who would live and fight together like brothers. A similar unit structure would much later be adopted by Rome.

Cyrus's attention to organizational detail is extraordinary when it's remembered that not many years before this, when Astyages's father organized the Median army into units, armies were simply a mass of men, all thrown together. Cyrus would apply the same eye for detail to the administration of his empire in the future. Having had so many years in service at Astyages's court before he came to power, he had the opportunity to observe the shortcomings in the way Astyages administered his military and his civil service.

Cyrus's father, Cambyses, had come to Hyrba to join his son. There is no mention of Cyrus's mother, Mandana, at this point; she drops out of his story once he set off to return to Anshan in the spring/summer of 552 BC and seems to have passed away during this period. Cambyses, by this time aged in his sixties, was, according to Ctesias, opposed to the Persian uprising. Herodotus's description of him as a quiet-tempered man proved true—it seems that all Cambyses wanted was an uncomplicated life full of comforts. Considering it madness to take on the much more numerous Medes, Cambyses counseled Cyrus to stop now, before Persis was destroyed. But as Cyrus would have pointed out, it was too late for both of them now; the damage had been done at Hyrba, and they had no choice but fight for their lives as well as for their people's freedom.

Cyrus appointed his reluctant father one of his generals and made his loyal lieutenant Oebares another. Then, as the winter snows began to melt in early 551 BC, Cyrus sent Oebares on a mission to the Persian mountain towns and villages to the north that would lie in the path of any advancing Median army. Oebares collected the populations of unprotected communities and relocated them to walled towns. He also created fortified watch posts overlooking mountain passes, manning them with small garrisons.

During the spring of 551 BC, Astyages advanced at a snail's pace down into Persis with a sprawling army of 220,000 men. They were commanded by leading Median nobles, including Harpagus and

Mazares, but Astyages wore the mantle of commander in chief. Each abandoned Persian town and village that Astyages encountered on the southward advance was looted and then burned to the ground. All the while, Cyrus's scouts and watch posts reported the progress of the vast Median army as it drew closer.

Repeatedly as he slowly advanced, Astyages sent messages to Cyrus and his father, threatening his grandson and son-in-law and ordering them to present themselves before him. If they came to them, he said, he would cast them into a dungeon in chains. "But if you are caught," he warned, "you will die a terrible death."[29]

Cyrus replied on behalf of his father and himself, declaring that the gods were on the Persians' side and advising Astyages to remove his forces from Persian soil and allow the Persians to be free. Ignoring his grandson's advice, Astyages drew closer with each passing day.

9

BATTLE OF THE BORDER

S WARMING OVER THE LAND like hungry locusts, a Median army
of 220,000 men approached a Persian city close to the border
with Media. No source names this city; it may have been Hyrba,
it may not. Certainly, Cyrus had been based in the city, waiting
with his forces for Astyages to come to him. Forewarned by his
outposts, he was ready.

With the Median vanguard still in the distance, the city gates
opened, and with precision, the Persian army marched out and
formed battle lines in front of the city. Cambyses took charge on
the right wing, Oebares on the left. Both were mounted. Cyrus,
who along with his staff was mounted, took up his position in the
center of the infantry line. He was accompanied, says Ctesias, by
"the Persian elite," members of his Achaemenid clan, and perhaps
the Immortals, his soon-to-be-famous infantry bodyguard unit.

The 10,000-Persian cavalry divided into two forces, which
took up positions on the outer flanks of the lines of some 40,000
Persian infantry. Most of the foot soldiers were light infantry
armed with javelins and daggers, or *scimitars*, Persian swords,

but one regiment of 10,000, probably the Immortals, was armed with heavy spears up to twelve feet long. Where Cyrus's one hundred new war chariots were positioned, we aren't told; they likely lined up in the center, in front of the infantry ranks.

Persians were notoriously dour in their food, habits, and dress, wearing simple, practical clothing in browns and black. This was in sharp contrast to the Medes, who dressed with color and ornamentation. Few Persians wore much protection. Writers spoke of the leather vests and breeches of the Persian rank and file of this era, and it's likely these men wore hardened leather that offered a measure of protection.

Cyrus's men didn't wear helmets either. The ordinary Persian foot soldier and cavalryman wore a distinctive woolen cap with a top that flopped over, a little like a tall beret. Under Cyrus and his successors, members of Persia's royal Achaemenid clan were permitted to wear firm caps that sat upright and were flat-topped, a cap similar to that of the Medes, except the Median cap had a round top. All Persian ranks used the distinctive Persian oval wicker shield, which had a half-moon section cut from each side, via which a man could protrude his javelin or sword when in close battle formation. In the fashion of the day, every single Persian wore a neat beard and mustache.

As the Median army formed up facing the vastly outnumbered Persians, King Astyages dismounted and took a seat on a throne set on a rise. From here, royal scepter in hand and a *kidaris* (the Median crown) on his head, he would watch the battle, surrounded by 20,000 bodyguard troops. He now gave orders for a force of 100,000 men to be detached, and sent them marching away. Once the remaining 100,000 men had lined up across the valley in their divisions of archers, spearmen, cavalry, and chariots, Astyages gave the order for the attack.

First, Median chariots swept forward and harassed the waiting Persians. Then the Median front line advanced in a full-frontal attack, leaving the bulk of the Median troops waiting in formation for their turn to be called forward. The first wave paused several times to launch arrows and then javelins and receive Persian arrows and javelins on their shields, then again charged forward. As Cyrus's troops waited to receive the charge, according to Xenophon they chanted a fierce battle hymn. A century and a half later, himself captaining Greek troops fighting the Persian army, Xenophon would hear the same chant.

It's likely that Cyrus's fearsome new war chariots now moved off, charging forward. But instead of veering away, they plunged into the surprised Medes, breaking their line. This allowed Cyrus and the Persian center to pour through the gaps and swing in behind the Median line. Attacking from front and rear, they annihilated the Medes. Time and again, Astyages sent new waves forward, and every time, the Persians slaughtered the attackers. Ctesias reports that "Cyrus and the rest of the Persians killed a great number of men."

Astyages, watching from his elevated throne, was furious—with the rebels and with his own men. He cursed and cried, "How valiant these pistachio-eating Persians are!" Sending messages to Harpagus and his other generals, he threatened them with fates worse than death if they failed to overcome the Persians.[30]

Cyrus would have been hoping that Harpagus would keep his word, given in the secret message the previous year, and defect to his side, or at least withdraw from the conflict. But Harpagus had specifically said that he and other Mede princes would change sides if and when Cyrus *invaded Media*; and right now, they were fighting on Persian soil. With no sign of Harpagus or any other Median general deserting Astyages, Cyrus knew that he was on his own.

The fighting seems to have become particularly heavy on the Persian right wing, where Cyrus's father was wounded. As yet another Median wave was bloodily repulsed, Cyrus could see that his men were struggling in the face of so many attackers. So, he led his battle lines in an orderly wheel away, toward the city. By day's end, he succeeded in getting the majority of his troops back behind the city walls, with the gates closing behind them. Astyages's troops made no attempt to follow. Instead, they fell back and made camp.

That night, in torchlight, Cyrus and Oebares both addressed their troops in the city. Stressing that the Persians had the better of the day's fighting, with many more Medians lying dead on the battlefield than Persians, the two Persian commanders declared that the next day their men must redouble their efforts and finally claim victory. Cyrus knew that it was make or break time. According to Ctesias, the rebel leader's words were somberly no-nonsense.

"We are all going to die sometime," Cyrus declared, "whether we are victorious or defeated tomorrow. So, if it must be, it's better to suffer death in victory, having set our homeland free."[31]

None of his listeners could have doubted the seriousness of the Persian situation when Cyrus then gave instructions for all women and children to leave the city in the night, taking only what they could carry, and flee east, higher into the mountains. Their objective was apparently a fort of the Pasargadae located on a conical hill on the bleak Morgab plain known today as Tall-e Takht, and which would become the foundation of the city of Pasargadae, Cyrus's later capital.

Cyrus bid a tearful farewell to his wife, Cassandana, and nine-year-old son, Cambyses. Cassandana, who would lead the women and children in their flight, was by this time again pregnant. With Astyages making no attempt to surround the city containing the Persian army, the Persian women and children all successfully made their escape, allowing Cyrus to concentrate on the upcoming resumption of hostilities.

The next day, before dawn, Cyrus had another tearful parting, this time with his father. While Cyrus and Oebares led the Persian fighting men out to do battle with the Medes for a second day running, the old men were to remain behind to defend the city, commanded by the wounded Cambyses. The father and son would never see each other again. With the dawn, the Persian fighting men marched from the city, full of anger and hatred toward the Medes, according to Ctesias, and once more formed up in their battle lines.

As battle resumed outside the city, Cyrus saw the force of 100,000 Medes detached by Astyages the previous day appear from the hills behind the city and quickly surround it. In danger of being caught between the two enemy forces, Cyrus instructed his army to disengage and make an ordered withdrawal via the mountains to Pasargadae. Oebares commanded a rearguard of 10,000 spearmen—probably the Immortals—which secured the narrow mountain passes and covered the withdrawal. Meanwhile as the Persians climbed the mountain paths to escape, out of necessity, all Cyrus's new chariots and a good many horses would have been abandoned; there was no place for them on the mountain slopes.

This left the few old and heavily outnumbered Persians defending the city with King Cambyses to their fate. Very soon the 100,000 attackers overwhelmed them, and the city fell. Cambyses was captured alive, although seriously wounded. Clapped in chains and threatened with being tortured to death, he was dragged from the city and taken to where King Astyages sat on his throne on the rise. Unceremoniously, he was thrown at the Median king's feet, as Astyages's generals Harpagus, Mazares, and others stood watching.

Elderly Astyages, now in his eighties and still disguising the ravages of age with a wig, eyeliner, and mascara, glowered down at Cambyses. "You were a good satrap for me, and I rewarded you," he declared. "Satrap" was the Persian title for a provincial governor. "And this is the thanks I get from you and your son!"

Cambyses, weak from his wounds, looked up at his father-in-law. "I don't know which of the gods it is that stirred up this madness in my son," he responded, "but don't you mistreat me! For, in my current state, I'll soon take my last breath in front of you."

"In that case," said Astyages, finding pity for his weakened son-in-law, "I shan't punish you at all. I know that if your son had listened to you, he wouldn't have done these things. So, I shall accord you a burial, since you didn't share this madness of his."[32]

Astyages was as good as his word. When Cyrus's father died shortly after this, Astyages, in remembrance of his daughter Mandana, had her Persian husband buried there on Persian soil with full funeral rights, although without marking the grave for future generations to find.

Then the Median king turned his attention, and his massed army, toward Pasargadae and the destruction of Cyrus and his rebels.

10

BATTLE OF PASARGADAE: THE FALL OF ASTYAGES

AT PASARGADAE, Cyrus and his troops regrouped and reunited with their women and children. Astyages, posting 100,000 men at the foot of the mountains, retired for the autumn and winter with plans to mount a fresh campaign against the bottled-up Persians come the following spring. This gave Cyrus and his men time to bind their wounds, replenish their supplies, and reequip for the next year's fighting. Later that year, Cassandana gave birth to Cyrus's first daughter, Atossa. In the coming few years, Cassandana would give Cyrus another son, Bardiya, and somewhat later, a second daughter, Roxane.

In the spring of 550 BC, Astyages and the Median army returned in force to resume the war against the Persian rebels. While Astyages made camp at the foot of the mountains, the Persians occupied the summit of the highest peak in the region. Astyages kept 50,000 men in the foothills, to intercept and kill both fleeing Persians and Median deserters, then sent the rest of his army, as many as 150,000 men, up the mountain slopes. As the Medians strove to climb narrow tracks via land that was sometimes heavily forested and often had steep drops, rebels harassed them every step of the way. Despite numerous casualties, the Median army pushed ever upward.

Leaving the women and children hiding at the summit, Cyrus and Oebares, reminding their men that their families were depending on them, led a fierce attack from the heights. When they ran out of ammunition, they rained stones down on the Medes, whooping their war cry. Ultimately, despite their courage, the heavily outnumbered rebels were pushed back, and Cyrus led his men in collecting their families and relocating to another peak.

According to Ctesias, that night Cyrus slept in the same mountain house that he'd stayed at during his time in the area as a youth. While he was making a sacrifice to the gods here, thunder rumbled and lightning flashed to his right, and auspicious birds—later events suggest they were falcons—settled on the roof of Cyrus's stone house. These were taken as signs that Cyrus had the favor of the Persian gods. That night, his troops prepared dinner and slept in the open. With the dawn, Cyrus and Oebares led a fresh assault on the Medes gathering below.

"Trust in the birds!" was the cry as the Persians came down from the heights, referring to the falcons that had settled on Cyrus's former home. The fighting was desperate, and at one time, a number of Persians fled back up to the summit, where the women and children were in hiding. According to Ctesias, women—the mothers of these men—raised their dresses, disgustedly baring their genitals to the deserters.

"Where are you off to, cowards?" the women demanded. "Do you want to crawl back where you came from?" By this they were sarcastically asking the men if they wanted to hide in the wombs that bore them.[33]

Hugely embarrassed, these men returned to the fight. Ctesias says that this episode led to a custom that was prevalent in his day, whereby, whenever the king of Persia visited Pasargadae, he would hand out gifts of gold coins to the women of the city, in remembrance of the women's role in what became known as the Battle of Pasargadae.

Running at the Medes in a last desperate charge, Cyrus and his reformed army drove the enemy off the mountain. In Ctesias's estimation, the battle had cost Astyages 60,000 men. Down in the lowlands at his base camp, a raging Astyages sent orders to his generals to redouble their efforts. But Harpagus, Mazares, and other Median commanders refused to continue leading their men against Cyrus. Finally, Harpagus kept his word to Cyrus. Withdrawing his allegiance from Astyages, he offered it to Cyrus. Even though the Medes still far outnumbered the Persians, Harpagus and his friends saw that the tide had turned for Cyrus. The Nabonidus Chronicle speaks of this officer-led Median mutiny as the end of Astyages's army.

As men fled from his camp all around him, throwing away their arms and heading for their homes across the empire, a shocked King Astyages realized that the battle was lost. It was "a shameful flight and dispersion of his army," says Herodotus. As for Astyages himself, not bothering to take any of his prized possessions with him, he mounted up and, traveling light, galloped away, heading north for Ecbatana on roads awash with deserters. A mounted entourage of staff and bodyguards hurried after him. According to the Babylonian Verse Account of Nabonidus, written during the reign of King Nabonidus, Babylonians were very much aware of the fate of the Median army at the hands of Cyrus: "Cyrus the king of Anshan (as Cyrus became on the death of his father), scattered the vast Median hordes with his small army."

Harpagus was now able to send a message up the mountain to Cyrus, telling him that he and his friends had changed sides and Astyages had abandoned his camp and was in flight. Warily, Cyrus and his men came down off the mountain and entered the vast, empty camp, which stood eerily silent with its thousands of deserted tents still containing the possessions and past booty of the Median army.

Harpagus, Mazares, and their fellow generals, waiting at Astyages's mighty tented pavilion, prostrated themselves before Cyrus. The victor strode past them and entered the king's tent, as his deputy Oebares, senior Persian officers, and bodyguards all crowded in after him. Astyages's throne, the one he'd previously occupied in the open, sat inside the tent. Beside it lay Astyages's royal scepter of state. Picking up the scepter, Cyrus tried the throne for size, as his men shouted their approval.

Oebares, taking up the *kidaris*, the Median crown, placed it on Cyrus's head, declaring, "You are worthier than Astyages to wear this. Bel is awarding it to you for your courage. And the Persians are worthier of ruling than the Medes."[34]

Cyrus gave Oebares the job of collecting all the treasures from the royal tents, and Oebares transported them up to Pasargadae and appointed men to guard them. The common soldiery was permitted by Cyrus to loot the rest of the Median camp; they would already be busy stripping the Median dead. As for Harpagus, Mazares, and the other Median generals, while other victors may have executed them, Cyrus not only spared them, he took them onto his staff. He did this even though they had only defected to him when it was clear that Median army morale had been shattered and Cyrus was on the verge of victory.

As previously mentioned, Cyrus seems to have given Harpagus his word that he would treat Medians as equals once he came to power, and despite what Oebares said about Persians being superior, Cyrus intended to stick to his undertaking. This attitude would come to be seen as immensely wise and magnanimous and proved the bedrock of Cyrus's power. He was, of course, half Median, half Persian, which helps explain his attitude. He may even have promised his Median mother, Mandana, that if he came to power, he wouldn't make slaves of the Medes.

Astyages, meanwhile, returned to Ecbatana, where he armed every man in the city, young and old alike.

"Cyrus will have no reason to rejoice," Astyages growled as he prepared to defend the city. At the same time, he ordered the arrest of all the surviving magi who, years before, had assured him that his dreams about Mandana had been realized by Cyrus's childhood game of kings. He had these magi crucified.[35]

Cyrus put Oebares in charge of the Persian army that now marched on Ecbatana. This army did battle with the ragtag Median force that Astyages brought out to defend the city. But Astyages's day of reckoning had come. "He was utterly defeated," says Herodotus, "his army being destroyed." After fleeing back into the city, Astyages was hidden in the royal palace by his younger daughter, Amytis, and her husband, Spitamas, governor of the home province of Media. Astyages's hiding place was apparently under the palace roof.

When Oebares strode into the palace, Harpagus accompanied him. Placing Amytis and Spitamas in chains, Oebares demanded to know where Astyages was hiding.

"We don't know anything about Astyages," Spitamas lied.[36]

So Oebares ordered the torture of Spitamas and Amytis, and then the torture of their sons, Spitaces and Megabernes, if they didn't reveal Astyages's hiding place. Astyages, hiding above, overheard this. To prevent his family members' torture, he called out, identifying where he'd concealed himself. Oebares ordered the old king brought down, then turned on Spitamas and had him put to death for lying to him. As for Amytis, Oebares ordered her treated with the respect due a mother. When Astyages was brought to him, he had manacles placed on his wrists and fetters on his ankles.

Harpagus now gloated over his king of the past thirty-five years. Confronting Astyages with gibes and jeers, he reminded him how he'd had his only son killed, cooked, and served to him for supper. "Now answer me this," Harpagus went on, "how do you enjoy being a slave instead of a king?"

Astyages may have lost his kingdom, but he hadn't lost his pride. Looking Harpagus full in the face, he retorted, "Why do you claim the achievements of Cyrus as your own?"

"Because it was my letter that made him revolt. So, I'm entitled to all the credit of the enterprise."

"In that case, you are the silliest and most unjust of men," Astyages declared. "Silliest because, if, when it was in your power to put the crown on your own head—as assuredly must have been the case if the revolt was entirely your doing—you placed it on someone else's head. (And you are) the most unjust of men, if, because of that one supper, you have brought slavery on the Medes."[37]

Before long, Cyrus himself entered Ecbatana and ordered Astyages and his daughter Amytis brought before him. No doubt to the consternation of Oebares and Harpagus, Cyrus ordered that Astyages be released from his chains, then announced that he was going to marry Amytis, his mother's now widowed younger sister and his aunt, making Astyages his father-in-law as well as his grandfather.

It was the norm for Persians to be polygamists, having multiple wives at the same time, plus concubines. Darius I, one of Cyrus's successors, would have seven wives and numerous concubines. Cyrus would only have the two wives, Cassandana and Amytis, with Cassandana being his love choice and Amytis his political choice. This way, no other man could marry Amytis and produce princes and princesses. At the same time, Cyrus's marriage to Amytis made her sons, Spitaces and Megabernes, his stepsons.

So now, Cyrus stood astride Persis and Media, uniting the two nations under his rule. Cassandana would continue to be the love of Cyrus's life, although Amytis would later bear a daughter to Cyrus, to be called Artystone. According to the Nabonidus Chronicle, Cyrus now sent the gold, silver, and other Median royal treasures to Anshan, the Persian capital. But he himself remained at Ecbatana for the immediate future, making it his administrative center. There, he took over the Median civil service of Astyages and molded it to his style and plans. He had never used eunuchs on his staff before, but for years, he'd worked closely with Astyages's eunuchs at the Ecbatana palace, and he now took four of them into his employ to run his civil service—Petisacas, Bagapates, Aspadates, and Izabates. The latter was, we know, an Egyptian. Ctesias says that Petisacas was to prove closest to Cyrus, serving as his chief of staff. Petisacas may in fact have been the eunuch who, three years before, set the Persian revolt in motion by convincing Astyages to let Cyrus go home to see his parents.

According to the Verse Account of Nabonidus, the Babylonians to the southwest soon learned of Astyages's fate at the hands of Cyrus: "He captured Astyages, the king of the Medes, and took him to his country as captive." However, for the time being Cyrus kept elderly Astyages close to him. Once all the lands that had been under Median control were brought into Cyrus's Persian Empire, he would send Astyages to Barcania, a territory adjacent to Media's Caspian Sea province of Hyrcania (Persian Verkana), to live in comfort but without power. This transfer to Barcania is likely to have come at the urging of Oebares, who apparently saw a living former ruler as a threat to Cyrus; while Astyages lived, he was a potential focus for rebellion. Amytis would harp at Cyrus to allow her father to return to court and be close to her, but for years to come, Cyrus would deny her requests.

While Media itself was now under Cyrus's dominion, the outlying nations that had been subjected to Median rule were yet to submit to him. This was to change relatively quickly. As soon as Artasyras, the Median governor of occupied Hyrcania, heard that Cyrus had defeated Astyages at the Battle of Pasargadae, he levied 50,000 local troops and marched south to Ecbatana. There, he prostrated himself at Cyrus's feet and swore allegiance to him, promising that he could raise another even larger army for him.

The Median governors of Parthia, Bactria, and the Sacae also vowed allegiance to Cyrus. However, the Bactrian people and the Sacian king Amorges had no desire to be subservient to Persians and saw this as an opportunity to make a bid for independence. Cyrus led an army against the Bactrians, apparently taking his new wife Amytis with him because the Bactrians held her in high regard. After the two evenly matched armies faced off, the Bactrians learned that Amytis was now Cyrus's wife and that Cyrus was treating her father with respect. As a result, they submitted to peace terms dictated by Cyrus.

When the Sacae rose up under Amorges, Cyrus marched against them. In the initial engagement, Cyrus captured Amorges. In response, Amorges's wife Sparethe raised an army of as many as 300,000 men and 200,000 women and surrounded one of Cyrus's armies, capturing its men, including its Median commander and his three sons. Ctesias identifies this commander as Parmises, brother of Amytis. However, Amytis had no brother that we know of. The captured commander may have been Artasyras the Mede; we hear nothing of him after the initial mention. Cyrus resolved the standoff with the Sacae via a negotiated truce, through which both sides returned their prisoners and hostilities were replaced by peace.

Even as Cyrus was bringing all Median territory to terms, a powerful nation to his northwest went to war with him.

11

A MIGHTY EMPIRE WILL
BE DESTROYED

CROESUS, SON OF KING ALYATTES, had ruled Lydia for ten years by the time that Cyrus took Ecbatana and dethroned Astyages. At forty-five, Croesus was five years younger than Cyrus. Croesus was, on the one hand, a wily king. Following his father's death, he had quickly and bloodily eliminated a rival, his half-brother Pantaleon, and eliminated Pantaleon's supporters. Croesus had also swiftly moved to consolidate Lydian power throughout Asia by sealing treaties with the Ionian Greek city-states of coastal Asia Minor, making them subservient to him and extending his control over a dozen of the most famous cities of the ancient Greek world.

Those city-states sent large annual tax payments to Croesus, swelling the treasuries in his capital, Sardis, which was already groaning with riches that Croesus's father had accumulated. King Alyattes was in fact credited with inventing silver and gold coinage. Lydia was rich in gold. Alluvial gold actually washed through Sardis via the Pactolus River, the waterway in which legendary

King Midas bathed in a vain attempt to rid himself of the power to turn everything he touched to gold.

Croesus's wealth was also legendary, leading to the saying, "As rich as Croesus." According to Plutarch, when the philosopher Solon of Athens visited Sardis at Croesus's invitation, to impress him Croesus had Solon shown through all the royal treasuries. When Solon came to the palace, he thought that every magnificently dressed, darkly bearded Lydian noble with hordes of guards and footboys he was introduced to must be Croesus. When Solon finally met the man himself, he found he was "decked with every possible rarity and curiosity, in ornaments of jewels, purple, and gold."[38]

Rich and politically astute he may have been, but Croesus was also deeply religious and anxious to be guided by the gods. A Greek ruler of a Greek nation, Croesus worshipped Zeus and the other Greek gods. Apollo—son of Zeus and the god of wisdom, the equivalent of the Babylonian god Nabu—was Croesus's patron deity. Apollo was also the god of prophesy, and throughout the Greek world and in Libya in North Africa, there were eight shrines to Apollo that boasted oracles offering prophetic answers to the questions of believers in exchange for donations. Croesus had come to rely on one of those oracles in particular.

Even before Croesus had become king, he had tested all eight oracles of Apollo to determine the most reliable. To each of the eight he had sent emissaries who, one hundred days after leaving Sardis, were to ask what Croesus was doing that very day. Having decided to do something totally unpredictable, on the hundredth day, Croesus cut up a tortoise and a lamb and boiled them in a brass cauldron.

To Croesus's astonishment, when his emissaries returned to report what the oracles had said, while most had failed the test, the oracular priestess at the Temple of Apollo at Delphi in western Greece, a priestess known as the Pythia and the Pythoness, had accurately told of the tortoise and lamb boiling in a brass cauldron. It apparently never occurred to Croesus that, before delivering a message from the Pythia, his emissaries to Delphi had perhaps bribed palace servants to tell them what Croesus had been doing on the hundredth day. Believing that Delphic Apollo was guiding him, from that day forward Croesus adopted the oracle of Delphi as his principal adviser, lavishing immensely rich gifts on the Delphic shrine.

When Croesus learned that Cyrus had overthrown Astyages, he quickly sent emissaries to Delphi, asking whether he should go to war with the Persians. If you remember, Croesus had married Astyages's sister Aryenis as part of the Lydian-Median peace deal following the Battle of the Eclipse, making Astyages Croesus's brother-in-law. No doubt, Croesus's wife now urged him to attack the Persians to rescue her brother, but in addition to this familial motive, Herodotus says that Croesus also had his eye on seizing Cappadocia, a state within the Median Empire that lay on his southeastern border.

In addition to asking the oracle whether he should confront Cyrus, Croesus also asked whether, if he were to go to war with the Persians, he should ally himself with another powerful Greek state. He already had treaties with the Egyptians and the Babylonians, but adding a particularly warlike Greek nation to his list of allies would make him feel all the more secure.

The Delphic Pythia subsequently replied: "If Croesus attacks the Persians, he will destroy a mighty empire." The oracle also advised him to determine the most powerful Greek states and ally himself with one of them. Delighted by these responses, Croesus sent a massive gift of gold coins to the people of Delphi by way of thanks for the oracle's guidance. Croesus funded this donation from the estate of his executed brother.[39]

In return, the grateful Delphians granted Croesus and all Lydians precedence whenever they sought predictions from the oracle.

This meant that when the Pythia conducted her monthly sessions beneath the Temple of Apollo, Lydians were ushered to the head of the line of supplicants that zigzagged down the hill path from the massive temple. Lydians were also exempted from all temple charges, given the best seats at Delphi's festivals, and granted the right to citizenship in the town of Delphi.

Despite the encouraging words from the oracle, Croesus was still nervous about going to war with Cyrus. Needing even more assurance of success, he sent again to Delphi, this time asking, "Will King Croesus's kingdom be of long duration?"

The reply came back from the Pythia:

> Wait 'till the time has come when a mule is monarch of Media;
> Then, you delicate Lydian, depart to the pebbles of Hermus;
> Hurry, oh, hurry away, and don't blush to behave like a coward.[40]

The Hermus was today's Gediz River in Anatolia. Known for its bed of limestone pebbles, it flowed west from the mountains to the Aegean Sea coast. Passing Sardis and entering the sea near the town of Phocaea, the river offered Croesus an escape route to the coast. Croesus laughed with relief when he received this message. It was, says Herodotus, the Delphic answer that pleased Croesus the most, "for it seemed incredible that a mule should ever become king of the Medes." As a result, Croesus concluded that neither he nor his descendants could ever lose the sovereignty of Lydia.

Croesus was in no hurry to go to war. This process of consulting the oracle at Delphi several times had taken a year or more. Next, Croesus consumed many more months on the subject of the recommended Greek alliance. After sending agents into Greece to discern the state of affairs there, reports led him to determine that it came down to two potential allies—the Athenians and the Lacedaemonians, or the Spartans as we know them.

Athens and Sparta were famed military powers and rivals, but Sparta then controlled most of the Peloponnese peninsula. Besides, when Sparta had some time back asked to buy a large quantity of gold from Croesus, he'd craftily let them have it for nothing, putting them in his debt. So Croesus sent emissaries to the Spartans. Seeing an alliance with Lydia as giving them the edge over all other Greek city-states, the Spartans quickly took the necessary oaths of friendship and alliance with Lydia, swearing by their common gods.

Sure of his ground now, Croesus finally committed to making war on the Persians. Planning to cross the Halys River and invade Cappadocia in the spring of 547 BC, he ordered the mass mobilization of Lydian mounted troops and the recruitment of large numbers of Greek mercenary foot soldiers from throughout the Greek states of Asia Minor. The Lydians were skilled horsemen and had a reputation for being among the best cavalry in the East. But a war could not be fought by cavalry alone. Infantry was also required, and this was where the paid Greek mercenaries would come in. The Greek hoplites fought in close formations bristling with twelve-foot spears that gave them the appearance of human hedgehogs.

As this military mobilization was underway, a Lydian noble named Sandanis urged Croesus to rethink his plan to make war on the Persians. He pointed out that the gods had not put it into Cyrus's mind to invade Lydian territory since conquering Media several years before, and he wondered if it was wise to attack him. Sandanis could not see what was to be gained by a war with the hard-living Persians, whereas wealthy Lydia had everything to lose. But Sandanis was wasting his breath. Croesus had made up his mind and could not be dissuaded from going to war. A tidal wave was rising, and nothing could divert it from its destructive course.

12

CROESUS VERSUS CYRUS

E VER SINCE TAKING ECBATANA, Cyrus hadn't contemplated
going to war with his powerful neighbors. To the contrary, busy
consolidating his rule of Media, he sent emissaries who sealed treaties
of friendship with Lydia and Babylon. This enabled him to focus on
administering his new Persian Empire. Maintaining the same basic
governing structure that had existed under the Medes, Cyrus made
Ecbatana his administrative headquarters and employed eunuchs
inherited from Astyages as his central administrators. Aramaic
became the language of the Persian bureaucracy—the same language
that would be spoken throughout the Middle East in the first century
and be the everyday language of Christ and his disciples.

Cyrus divided his empire into provinces and appointed governors. As he seems to have guaranteed Harpagus at the outset
of the Persian revolt, he treated Medes as the equals of Persians
in every respect. Median nobles including Harpagus and Mazares were numbered among his counselors, alongside his Persian
deputy Oebares. In the same way, the provincial governors Cyrus
appointed were a mixture of Persians and Medes.

These governors were called satraps, and the provinces, satrapies. Each satrapy was semi-autonomous. It was expected to send taxes to Ecbatana and to supply troops. Otherwise, each satrap ran his province with a good deal of autonomy. Nonetheless, Cyrus knew that this could lead to oppression and corruption, so he appointed an inspector-general, a man called the King's Eye. This official, who reported directly to Cyrus, did an annual inspection of every province. Should the King's Eye find anything untoward in a province, he had the authority to order the satrap to put things right. And if the satrap didn't comply, the King's Eye went straight to Cyrus.

In addition, says Xenophon, Cyrus personally appointed and dismissed the captains of the guard units stationed in the citadel of every city throughout his empire and published the names of his senior officials and guard captains in a Royal List. To keep in close touch with his satraps, Cyrus established a government courier system, a pony express, with horse-changing stations set up no more than a day's ride apart from one end of his empire to the other. As the Persian Empire expanded, so too did this courier service. Rome's first emperor, Augustus, would 450 years later set up a similar government courier system, the Cursus Publicus Velox (literally, the state's very fast runner). Augustus would boast that messages from the farthest fringes of his empire would take no more than ten days to reach him via this system. It was Cyrus's model for this efficient courier service that the Romans would adopt.

Most of the Persian troops who'd helped Cyrus conquer Astyages were sent home to their farms, stock runs, cities, and villages. The best and bravest of them, probably men of the Pasargadae tribe, were retained for the Immortals, Cyrus's permanent 10,000-man bodyguard. The unit, which now also included the best Median troops, was to gain its name from the fact that its complement was never allowed to fall below 10,000; it was as if the unit was immortal. Should a man fall in battle or be invalided out through wound, injury, or infirmity, a replacement was immediately shunted in to take his place. By implication, this suggests that another associated unit must have existed to train candidates who could immediately be used as Immortals replacements. According to Xenophon, all 10,000 men of the Immortals were spearmen, men whose principal weapon was the javelin.

Cyrus, having spent so many years at the Median court, and having a Median mother, soon adopted Median color and ostentation into his style of dress, which included necklaces and earrings, and his Persian nobles followed suit. According to Xenophon, in military mode, Cyrus and his staff would now wear scarlet tunics, bronze breastplates of Egyptian design, and bronze helmets with white plumes. Their weapons were a short sword on the belt, plus, in the hand, a heavy javelin made from tough and resilient cornel-wood. A stone engraving confirms that Cyrus indeed wore an elaborate helmet for ceremonial occasions, a helmet from which projected the horns of a bull—in honor of Mithra. Xenophon says the armor and fittings of Cyrus's attendants shone with a veneer of gold, while that of Cyrus himself glowed with solid gold.

Cyrus never took his eyes off his neighbors all this time. He knew that Lydia and Babylon were linked by treaty, and he could guess that both were worried by their new Persian neighbors. Xenophon says that Cyrus made a habit of sending spies into foreign territory, often disguised as runaway slaves, and these would have reported back by 548 BC that King Croesus of Lydia was mobilizing Lydian cavalry and recruiting an army of Greek mercenaries.

Cyrus's response was to send envoys to the Ionian Greek cities that lined the Aegean coast of Asia, proposing alliances with them—alliances that meant they would not support Lydia in any conflict with Cyrus. All but one of those Ionian cities rebuffed Cyrus's advances and reaffirmed their support of Lydia. The exception was the city of Miletus in Caria, today's western Anatolia. The Miletus agreed to a peace pact with Cyrus and would henceforth stay out of the war that Croesus was planning to wage on the Persians.

It would have been no surprise to Cyrus when reports reached him in the spring of 547 BC that a Lydian army was massing at the Halys River, the border between Lydia and the north of the Persian province of Cappadocia. Crossing the broad, deep Halys to enter Cappadocia was to prove no easy thing. Herodotus was told that the problem was solved for Croesus by noted Greek astronomer and engineer Thales of Miletus, who supervised the diversion of the river from in front of the encamped Lydian army to behind it. Herodotus was loathe to believe this, as there was no report of the river again being diverted when the Lydian army later returned to the western bank. Bridges spanned the Halys when Herodotus visited the site a century later, and he was of the view that Croesus had them built for his 547 BC crossings.

Once Croesus's army crossed to the eastern side of the river, it entered the northern Cappadocian district of Pteria. The district capital, also named Pteria, lay near the Black Sea city of Sinope, in what was to become known in Roman times as Pontus. The walled city of Pteria occupied a rise and was the strongest position in the district. As the Lydian invaders approached, ravaging wheat fields and villages, the local Cappadocians, whom the Greeks called White Syrians, fled to the safety of the city, and the gates were closed. Croesus pitched camp outside the city and surrounded Pteria, putting it under siege.

In Ecbatana, when word reached Cyrus that the Lydians had invaded, he calmly issued orders for a Persian army to be formed for a counter-offensive, making careful plans for the operation. Cyrus even dictated the order of march for his army, giving much attention to his baggage trains. For one thing, with horses and other baggage animals in short supply, he acquired camels from Arab traders and added them to his other baggage trains. He also created separate baggage animals for each regiment, to carry their tents and supplies, and placed each baggage train with its regiment in the column of march. In this way, several baggage trains were salted through a marching column, where they were protected, rather than have one large baggage train trail behind the army and become a tempting target for the enemy.

The Romans would call an army's trundling baggage train the impedimenta, and it could indeed become an impediment to an impatient general. Roman general Mark Antony was to learn the hard way that it was imperative to protect your baggage on the march. In 36 BC, leading four legions into Parthia, he left the baggage train to follow as he pushed on ahead with the fighting troops. Parthian cavalry simply circled around behind the legions and sacked their baggage. Without water, supplies, and ammunition, Antony was forced to make a harrowing fighting retreat, with many of his men perishing in the process.[41]

Cyrus even dictated the precise location of each element of his army in the camp made at the end of each day's march. Radiating from his pavilion were to be the tents of his staff, his cooks, his bakers, then those of each regiment. Every time the army camped for the night, Cyrus's troops would know exactly where to locate and erect their tents. And should Cyrus need to send for a particular commander in the night, his messengers knew precisely where to find that officer's tent.

Xenophon says that Cyrus gave each Persian regimental commander an individual standard, and on the march and in battle the commander's body servant carried it at the head of the regiment. Using Cyrus's personal standard as a guide, these standards took the form of a square cloth flag held aloft on a spear shaft. We don't know what motifs these standards used, but again, based on Cyrus's standard, they would have represented animals sacred to the Persians, such as the dog, raven, scorpion, snake, lion, and griffin/dragon.

Xenophon describes Cyrus's own ensign as follows: "The standard was a golden eagle, with outspread wings, borne aloft on a long spear-shaft." Rather than an eagle, we know that it was in fact a falcon, a similar bird of prey to the eagle. The Persians called Cyrus's symbol the *Shahbaz*, the royal falcon, and it was based on a fabled falcon, a god of the mountains Persians called upon in times of trouble. In all likelihood, Cyrus chose the falcon as his emblem because the birds that had alighted on his quarters just prior to his victory in the Battle of Pasargadae had been falcons.

Cyrus's flag is likely to have had a scarlet background. Cyrus and his personal staff all wore scarlet tunics; red was the easiest and cheapest color to obtain in those times. From engravings, we know that above the head of Cyrus's spread-eagle falcon in his symbol there was an orb, representing Mithra. The sacred bird clutched another orb in each of its claws, representing the sun and the moon. Xenophon says that Cyrus's *Shahbaz* emblem was still being used by the kings of Persia a century and a half after Cyrus's death.

The Lydian siege of Pteria lasted some months, and during that time, Croesus was content to sit in camp and wait. This gave Cyrus all the time he needed to organize his army. When he set off northwest, it was the autumn of 457 BC. He marched, says Herodotus, "increasing his numbers at every step by the forces of the nations that lay in his way." According to Ctesias, those forces included a contingent from the Sacae led by their king, Amorges. They would also have included the Hyrcanians previously volunteered by Artasyras, as well as Persian and Median troops.

Some modern historians have concluded that the army Cyrus took against Croesus was small compared to Croesus's forces, but given the time he had to assemble it, and the fact that Herodotus explicitly states that Cyrus's army outnumbered that of Croesus, it is highly unlikely that the Persian army was anything but large. As for Croesus's army, Xenophon numbered it at 420,000 and wrote that elements of it were made up of 120,000 Egyptians who joined Croesus by sea, 60,000 Babylonians, and Arabians. This is all highly suspect. While we know Croesus had alliances with the Pharaoh of Egypt and king of Babylon, no other classical author mentions Egyptian or Babylonian troops marching for Croesus, and it's most unlikely they were involved. As for Arabian troops, they would have had to cross Babylonia to reach Lydia, and the Babylonian king was unlikely to have permitted that.

Croesus's treaties with other nations were defensive in nature. Like defense treaties today, they required one party to come to the aid of the other if it came under attack. Croesus's Cappadocian campaign was an offensive one, not a defensive one; he was invading Persian territory. Would the rulers of Egypt, Babylon, and Arabia really have marched with Croesus against Persia on Persian soil, making Cyrus their enemy? Subsequent events indicate otherwise. We do know that later, only once Croesus was back on Lydian soil, he did invoke his defense treaties with allies.

Caria was one of the Greek nations in league with Croesus. The Carians were noted mercenary fighters who provided infantry to the highest bidders, including the Pharaoh of Egypt. There were even Carian military colonies near Memphis, the Egyptian capital, inhabited by Carian military veterans. Herodotus says the Carians reputedly invented handles for shields—previously shields had been slung over the left shoulder—and were the first to paint motifs on shields. Likewise, they had invented helmet crests; the Persians nicknamed the Carians "Cocks" as a consequence. Carians were marching for Croesus, and it's equally likely that some of these men had served the pharaoh. Perhaps Xenophon had received a garbled reference to these men who had served in Egypt and turned them into 120,000 fictional Egyptian troops.

Xenophon again gives both sides chariots for this battle—while other authors do confirm that Cyrus used chariots against the Medes, there is no mention of Persian chariots by the time Cyrus went against Croesus. Xenophon also puts a force of camel-mounted archers on Cyrus's side at this point; however, as will be seen, camels were involved in a later battle, not at Pteria, and even then, without archers.

Everything points to Cyrus and his army reaching Pteria by October. His commanders included his deputy Oebares as well as an otherwise unknown Persian noble identified as Adousius by Xenophon, and another, Hystaspes—called Hystaspas by Xenophon. We know quite a lot about Hystaspes. Like Cyrus, he was descended from Achaemenes and Teispes, making Hystaspes and Cyrus distant cousins. According to Xenophon, for this campaign, Cyrus appointed Hystaspes commander of one of the two wings of his cavalry. Harpagus the Mede was also marching with Cyrus, probably in command of a Median contingent.

Outside the city of Pteria, Cyrus made camp within sight of Croesus's forces. By this time the city had fallen to Croesus, apparently forced to surrender due to starvation rather than falling by storm to the Lydians. Croesus had made every man, woman, and child in Pteria a slave, and by the time Cyrus arrived, these Cappadocians seem to have been sent back across the Halys to Lydia. Croesus had made no attempt to advance farther into Persian territory. Instead, he would have allowed his troops, especially his mercenaries, to enrich themselves by looting Pteria. He seems to have been content to wait, drawing Cyrus to him.

With the Persian army encamped across the plain, Croesus formed up his army to offer battle. Unlike the Persian rank and file, the Lydians and their Greek allies all wore helmets. The mercenary infantry took up their positions in the center of Croesus's battle formation, with the Lydian cavalry on each wing. Herodotus tells us only a little about the Battle of Pteria. Ctesias tells us nothing. Xenophon tells us a great deal, but sadly, it reads like a Marvel Comics rendition of an ancient battle, with extravagant speeches, corny macho dialogue, exciting over-the-top heroic action scenes, and even a love story subplot. Overall, Xenophon's account is clearly fictitious. Perhaps some basic elements of the battle were relayed to him by a Persian source, but the rest belongs in the pulp fiction category.

Basically Xenophon says that Cyrus formed his army into a box formation, with 2,000 reserves in the rear, hoping to lure the Lydians into attempting to envelop his flanks. As usual, Cyrus divided his cavalry over the two wings, with Hystaspes commanding cavalry on the Persian left. When the Lydians took the bait and swung troops around his flanks, says Xenophon, Cyrus charged Croesus's center, where the mounted Croesus was located. This charge broke through opposition ranks. Xenophon invents the tale that Croesus's isolated Egyptian troops parleyed and agreed to change sides to fight for Cyrus, but only on the condition that they didn't have to fight Croesus and the Lydians. As previously pointed out, it's unlikely any Egyptian troops were present, and there is no record of Egyptians subsequently marching for Cyrus.

From Herodotus, we learn that the Battle of Pteria lasted all day. Hostilities were broken off at nightfall, with neither side having gained an advantage. "The combat was hot and bloody," says Herodotus, "and on both sides the number of slain was great." Leaving the battlefield littered with their dead, the two armies withdrew to their camps for the night, taking their wounded with them. According to Herodotus, Croesus blamed his lack of victory on the fact that Cyrus's forces outnumbered his own. When Cyrus didn't lead his army out of camp the following day to resume hostilities, Croesus followed suit.

That night, says Xenophon, Croesus executed a strategic withdrawal. No doubt he left much of his camp intact to distract the Persians, for there is no report of Cyrus's troops attempting to prevent the Lydian pullout or harassing their withdrawal or their recrossing of the Halys. Cyrus would have let his men loot the abandoned enemy camp as a reward for their valiant fighting. So, the Lydians retreated from Cappadocia and went home.

Not that Croesus saw this as a defeat. By early November, back in his capital, Sardis, he was all the more determined to conquer the Persians. With that in mind, and certain that Cyrus would mount an invasion of Lydia come the spring, Croesus sent emissaries hurrying to Egypt, Babylon, and Sparta, activating his treaties with all three and calling on them to send armies to meet him at Sardis five months from the date of the emissaries' departure from Sardis. His plan was for a joint "defensive" campaign against the Persians in the spring. In the meantime, Croesus paid off his mercenary troops and sent them home, giving them orders to return to Sardis at the start of the following spring.

As Croesus settled down to wait out the winter, he received reports that masses of snakes were invading the pastures outside the city where the thousands of Lydian warhorses were grazing, attacking the steeds. In all probability, the Sardis region had experienced a prolonged dry spell that summer and fall, and the watering of the now-returned warhorses had attracted the snakes. But superstitious Croesus wondered if there was a supernatural meaning to the snake invasion, a warning of some kind from the gods. So, he determined to seek guidance.

With time and winter weather against sending his emissaries across the sea to Delphi, Croesus dispatched them overland to nearby Telmessos, a city in western Lydia near the border with Caria that was home to a school of famous diviners of omens and messages from the gods. Croesus asked the Telmessian soothsayers to tell him what, if anything, this snake event presaged.

And then, just a day or two later, a panicky message reached Croesus: Cyrus was approaching, personally leading a Persian cavalry vanguard, while behind him, the entire Persian army was advancing with its baggage trains. Croesus had imagined that, like himself and like every other general, Cyrus would have retired for the winter, to resume fighting in the spring. But Cyrus was more tactically astute than that—much more.

Opportunity is like virginity; once lost, it can never be regained.

Seeing the opportunity to catch his opponent unprepared, Cyrus had crossed the Halys in Croesus's wake. Now, it dawned on Croesus that he'd been outwitted by the Persian. And it was too late to recall the discharged mercenaries. Just the same, Croesus was no coward. Immediately, he ordered the call to arms sounded for the Lydian cavalry, and he prepared to lead his men out to face the approaching enemy.

Days later, too late, the messengers would return from Telmessos with the answer to Croesus's question to the diviners of omens. "Look for the entry of an army of foreign invaders into your country," they would warn.[42] Not that the Telmessian warning would have made any difference to what was about to transpire, even if Croesus had received it in time. His destiny was now in the hands of Cyrus.

13

SARDIS: THE FALLEN HELMET

THE PLAIN AROUND SARDIS was flat and treeless. A number of
streams that watered the plain and made it fine agricultural
land ran into the Hermus River. Across these flatlands marched
the Persian army, to make camp within sight of the tall stone walls
of the famously opulent Lydian capital, whose citadel sat on a high
stone promontory that rose up from the flat plain. As it did so,
the Lydian army formed up outside the city—an army made up
entirely of cavalry.

Cyrus promptly called together his council of advisers.
How many advisers made up his royal inner sanctum, we don't
know, but several decades later, Cyrus's successor Darius I, son
of Cyrus's general Hystaspes, who favored the sacred number
seven in many things, used a council of seven. Cyrus frequently
consulted his advisers. We are told that he would listen as each
asserted his viewpoint and then make a decision. Consensus
formed no part of Cyrus's decision-making. Even when a majority of counselors were agreed on something, Cyrus would some-

times take on board the contrary opinion of a single adviser if he thought it the wisest course of action. In this meeting on the approaches to Sardis, Cyrus adopted a suggestion put forward by Harpagus the Mede.

Up to this point, while Cyrus had kept Harpagus close, he had refrained from giving him major responsibilities. Cyrus had never forgotten that, while the Median army mutiny led by Harpagus at the time of the Battle of Pasargadae had inspired the ultimate defeat of Astyages, Harpagus had only defected to him at the last moment, when Cyrus looked likely to win the battle anyway. Conscious of the fact that an opportunist who betrays one leader can betray another, Cyrus had yet to trust Harpagus completely. But Harpagus had come up with an idea that would improve his stock with his Persian master.

Fighting an enemy who exclusively fielded cavalry called for different tactics than those applied to a battle against an army made up primarily of infantry. Cavalry were much more mobile and could move about a battlefield, charging opposing forces here, nipping in and out in hit-and-run attacks there, and rapidly outflanking opposition infantry. However, Harpagus knew that horses were spooked by the sight and smell of camels. And there were a number of camels in the Persian baggage trains. Perhaps the horses of Harpagus's own Median cavalry had been unsettled on the march northwest by the presence of camels in the Persian column, and this gave him the idea.

Harpagus therefore suggested that the camels be placed at the front of the Persian advance, to spook the Lydian horses. Cyrus thought this an excellent idea. So, the provisions the camels carried were offloaded, and men equipped as cavalrymen mounted the beasts. The camels were then brought to the front of the Persian column, and as Cyrus's army formed up across the plain, the new camel corps deployed in front of the infantry as the cavalry took its regular post on the two wings. Cyrus himself was mounted in the center with his staff, with his standard-bearer proudly holding aloft the fluttering *Shahbaz* standard.

Cyrus now had a general order transmitted throughout his army by mounted heralds: "Slay every Lydian who comes in your way, without mercy. But spare Croesus. Don't kill him, even if he should be seized and offer resistance."[43] He then gave the order for the advance.

Across the plain, Croesus and his thousands of cavalrymen waited outside the suburbs of Sardis, with Croesus probably flying the standard of a lion, an animal that was prominent in Lydian mythology. With their horses pawing the ground, the Lydian troopers held their long lances high, waiting for the order to charge. When that order came, they would lower their lances, projecting them out beyond their steeds' heads. But as the Persian army drew closer and the Lydian horses, well-groomed animals carrying armor on their chests and heads, caught the scent of the camels on the breeze, they became uneasy. Soon, as camels came nearer, restless horses became unmanageable, and then they were turning and bolting for the rear in terror.

Many Lydian riders were either thrown off their horses or dismounted. Herodotus says that the Lydians were brave men and famous warriors. Even though they had lost their mounts, and even as clouds of Persian arrows filled the air, many cavalrymen joined their king in drawing their swords and closing on the Persians to fight on foot. There was great slaughter on both sides that day, says Herodotus. But the Lydians suffered the worst. Croesus's hopes, says Herodotus, withered away, and before long, he made a fighting retreat to the city. His surviving men fled to join him. The gates of the city, a city that according to legend had been founded by the sons of classical hero Hercules, thudded closed, and the Persians were left in command of the field.

Cyrus ordered camp made and gave directions for entrenchments to be built all the way around Sardis, beyond bow range, sealing off the city from the outside world. That night, before Sardis could be fully encircled, Croesus had riders slip out a gate and ride away. They bore messages for his allies, including the Spartans, begging them to come at once to his aid. Cyrus fully expected the siege of Sardis to last for months. Croesus, for his part, believed he had sufficient supplies to hold out for some time, certainly until his allies arrived to relieve the siege.

But Cyrus was loathe to tie down his entire army here. There was always the possibility that the Greek mercenaries would mobilize and return to help their former employer. This possibility was driven home to him when messengers arrived from Caria. The citizens of an unnamed Carian city, probably its capital Halicarnassus, today's Turkish city of Bodrum, were split over whether or not they should help Croesus. The pro-Persian faction now sought Cyrus's aid.

So, says Xenophon, Cyrus detached part of his army from the siege, and putting them under the command of Adousius, sent them marching away to Halicarnassus. In all likelihood, these troops pulled out in the night, to ensure that Croesus was unaware that they had gone. According to Ctesias, Cyrus's deputy Oebares came up with a cunning ploy designed to deceive the Lydians into believing that the entire Persian army continued to occupy the trenches now surrounding Sardis. For there was always the danger that, realizing that surrounding enemy troop numbers had been reduced, Croesus might attempt a breakout.

Oebares's scheme involved the creation of a ghost army of Persian soldiers. Built on wooden cross-frames, wearing Persian clothing, caps, and even false beards, armed with spare spears, bows, and quivers, these dummy soldiers were installed overnight among the remaining real troops. When the sun rose, from the city walls there appeared to be the same number of Persian troops in the distant trenches as before. As long as the real troops moved about now and then, the illusion could be maintained.

This crafty trick worked so well that Cyrus sent another detachment of troops, this one under Hystaspes's command, into Phrygia to bring it under Persian control. Once these troops had also slipped away, more dummies fooled the Lydians into believing that the entire Persian army continued to surround Sardis.

As the days of the siege passed monotonously, Cyrus was forced to sit and do nothing, and he became increasingly impatient. After two weeks, he sent heralds riding around his entrenchments to read out a proclamation: "To the man who first mounts the city wall, I promise a great reward."[44]

One of the thousands of men who heard this proclamation was a Persian soldier by the name of Hyroeades, a member of the Marsi tribe. According to Xenophon, this man had formerly been a slave in the service of a Lydian officer of the permanent guard in Sardis's hilltop citadel, and as a result, he was familiar with the city layout. Hyroeades's post in the Persian entrenchments faced a seemingly sheer precipice, which formed part of the city defenses on the western, Hermus River side of Sardis.

According to myth, a past king of Sardis, Meles, had sent to the soothsayers of Telmessos asking how he could make the city safe from attack. According to the myth, the Telmessians, aware that one of King Meles's concubines had just given birth to a lion, had advised Meles to carry the lion cub around the circuit of the city's defenses, which would render the city impregnable. This Meles had done, with the exception of the side where the sheer rock rose up to form a natural part of the city wall. As far as Meles was concerned, the precipice made this part of the defenses of Sardis absolutely secure, and for this reason, he'd not carried the lion past it.

It so happened that, the day before Cyrus offered the reward to his men, Hyroeades the soldier had witnessed an interesting occurrence. While on watch in the trenches, with members of the ghost army for company, he had seen a helmet tumble down the precipice from the top. A Lydian soldier had scuttled after the helmet, intent on reclaiming it before his officer punished him for losing it. To Hyroeades's amazement, the Lydian followed a rough natural path down the escarpment, a path that was invisible from below. Unaware that he was being watched, the Lydian retrieved his helmet and scrambled back up to the top.

Once darkness fell, Hyroeades scurried across no-man's-land and began to climb the slope. He must have told friends what he had witnessed and what he intended doing, for a number of other Persian soldiers quickly followed his example. It was probably a moonlit night as Hyroeades and those who came after him carefully climbed the hidden path up the precipice.

Eventually, Hyroeades achieved the impossible and found himself inside Sardis's citadel, which housed King Croesus and his bodyguards. Soon joined by comrades, Hyroeades seems to have opened a city gate from within, and more Persian troops streamed inside. Whether or not Hyroeades received the promised reward from Cyrus for being the first over the city wall, we aren't told, but the fact his name was recorded and passed along to Herodotus suggests he was. Once Persian troops were inside the city, Sardis quickly and easily fell. Within the royal palace, Croesus was woken with the news that the Persians were in the city. He quickly dressed and, accompanied by his youngest son, hurried to investigate.

Herodotus tells us that a Persian soldier ran at Croesus with his weapon raised. As he did, Croesus's youngest son and heir—his eldest boy had years before been killed in a hunting accident—stepped into his path.

"Man," cried the youth, "don't kill Croesus!" This saved the king's life. It was all the more amazing because the youth had never before spoken a word in his life and was assumed to be dumb.[45]

Cyrus's deputy Oebares now entered the city. Taking charge, he had Croesus placed in manacles and fetters and had him, together with his wife, son, and some retainers, lodged in the inner sanctum of Sardis's Temple of Apollo. Ctesias says that Oebares put a heavy guard over the locked temple door to keep the captured king contained.

There Croesus was meant to stay while Oebares terminated all Lydian resistance in the city, with Cyrus remaining outside Sardis until his deputy had everything under control. But three times that night, according to Ctesias, Croesus escaped unseen from the temple, perhaps via a secret tunnel linking it with the palace. He was recaptured in the city each time. According to Ctesias, the Lydian men with Croesus were beheaded for facilitating and covering up his escapes, among them Croesus's son; he also claims that, after Croesus's wife saw her sole remaining boy killed before her eyes, she threw herself from the city wall, taking her own life. However, another story has both Croesus's son and wife still alive the following day, and the more credible Herodotus says the boy was to live for a number of years after this and retained the power of speech for the remainder of his life.

Come Croesus's third recapture, it was daylight. It was only then, says Xenophon, that Cyrus entered the city. According to Herodotus, Cyrus issued an order, an order that was totally out of character from the Cyrus we otherwise know; never before had he issued such a brutal order, and never would he do so again. Lumber was brought, and a massive pyre created, where the troublesome king was to be burned to death. Why? Perhaps the notoriously tricky Croesus had given his word, sworn on oath to his gods, that he would not attempt escape, in which case he'd broken his word three times and lost all claim to mercy because of repeatedly breaking his sacred oath.

Herodotus also tells us that, not only was Croesus condemned to a fiery death, two groups of seven sons of Lydian nobles were sentenced to die with him on the pyre. Certainly, the story that was told to Herodotus, attributing this execution order to Cyrus, troubled the historian, for it left him scratching his head for a motive.

"I don't know whether Cyrus had in mind making a [sacrificial] offering of the first-fruits [of victory] to some god or other," Herodotus wrote, "or whether he'd taken a vow and was keeping it; or whether he'd heard that Croesus was a religious man and wanted to see if any of the heavenly powers would appear to save him from being burnt alive."

This intended execution of a captured ruler is so at odds with what we know about Cyrus that some scholars such as noted Austrian historian Reinhold Bichler suspect that here Herodotus's Lydian source was in error—Herodotus tells us his sources for the story of Croesus's reign were Lydians. Perhaps the Lydian sources wanted to cast the blame on the Persian king. Bichler suggests that such a gruesome death was not ordered by Cyrus at all, but by the likes of his Median general Harpagus, before Cyrus entered the city.[46]

Cyrus's Persian deputy Oebares, meanwhile, was to demonstrate a keenness to eliminate any former sovereign whose existence he perceived to pose a threat to his lord and master. As Oebares had a key role in the command of the siege and was inside the city when Croesus was captured, it's possible the king's execution order came from him. Another strong possibility is that the sentence was actually passed by the Persian royal judges, the *databara* or law-bearers, who accompanied Cyrus, and he was bound by Persian law to abide by the sentence. Two decades later, the databara would levy a similarly harsh multiple-death sentence in Egypt after Persian envoys were massacred while bearing the symbol of peace.

Whoever ordered the execution, preparations went forward. The pyre was made ready on an elevated part of the citadel of Sardis, overlooking the city, with neatly stepped timbers rising a number of feet, like stairs, to the small platform at the top, where a wooden throne taken from Croesus's palace was placed. King Croesus and his fourteen fellow victims, the sons of Lydian nobles, were led out in chains.

14

KILLING A KING

MOST ANCIENT ACCOUNTS of the execution of Croesus imply that it was set to take place the day after the Lydian king's capture. Yet, one account has weeping women throughout Lydia preparing the robes Croesus was to wear at his execution—meaning that between his capture and the day of execution there was a period of days or weeks to allow this to occur, which was probably not the case.

Herodotus tells us that during that day, the skies had been clear and there was not a breath of wind, although, as the execution got underway, dark clouds were quickly forming overhead. After Croesus was led out, he went through a tearful parting from his wife and son. The boy had to be dragged from his father's arms. The Persian guards then led the king to the top of the pyre and chained him in place on his throne. An ancient Greek amphora bearing an image of Croesus on the pyre shows him sitting barefoot on his throne, wearing flowing robes and a leafy crown and holding a disc and scepter, symbols of his reign, a reign that was about to end in flames, as a Persian in ceremonial dress lights the pyre.

Cyrus was watching, perhaps from a throne of his own, and as the fire was lit, he heard Croesus call out.

"Solon! Solon! Solon!"[47]

Unable to understand what Croesus had said, Cyrus sent interpreters who called to Croesus as the wood at the fringes of the pyre began to ignite, asking what he had meant by "Solon! Solon! Solon!" Croesus didn't immediately reply, but as the interpreters pressed him, he told them of the visit he had received from the philosopher Solon of Athens some years before. After Croesus had displayed his vast riches to his guest, he'd asked Solon who he thought the man who led the happiest life must be, expecting Solon to name him. Solon had instead named an Athenian who had happily died in battle for his country. So Croesus had asked who the second happiest man must be, again expecting to be named. This time, Solon had named two poor brothers who had happily harnessed themselves to their mother's wagon and died under the strain.

Croesus, furious with these answers, had wanted to know why, with all his riches, he shouldn't be considered the man who led the happiest life. Solon had replied that fortunes can change, and Croesus should wait before he made such a claim. "To salute as happy one that is still in the middle of life and hazard," Solon had told him, "is about as safe and conclusive as crowning and proclaiming as victorious the wrestler who isn't yet in the ring."[48]

At the time of Solon's visit, Croesus had thought the philosopher an idiot. Now, with all his riches useless to him and about to die a far from happy death, Croesus realized how vain, smug, and naive he had been to boast of his wealth, and how right Solon had been. By the time the interpreters returned to Cyrus and relayed Croesus's explanation, flames had begun to lick higher on the pyre.

Ancient commentators gave Cyrus credit for realizing that, as the fire's intensity grew, there but for the grace of the gods went he. This realization, and the fact that Croesus seemed to have gained humility in his last minutes of life, are said to have combined to cause Cyrus to decide that such a man did not deserve to die. It is possible that Cyrus was looking for an excuse to overrule his judges or his loyal deputy Oebares; if this was case, Croesus had given him the excuse he needed. Cyrus ordered Croesus and the boys spared and taken from the pyre.

Saving Croesus was easier said than done. The growing flames made it impossible for Cyrus's attendants to reach Croesus and the boys, as hard as they tried. As men ran to fetch water in jars to douse the fire, Croesus, feeling his predicament hopeless, looked to the black sky above and begged his patron deity Apollo to rescue him.

"If you ever received a gift from me that was acceptable," Croesus wailed to the heavens, "I beg you, come to my aid and deliver me from my present danger."[49]

Almost at once, from the black clouds overhead, a storm broke, and rain fell so thickly that it put out much of the fire and allowed Croesus and the boys to be plucked from the top of the pyre. Singed but alive, Croesus was brought before Cyrus. Of course, ancient Greek authors credited Apollo's intervention for Croesus's escape from death.

Cyrus, meanwhile, had some questions for Croesus. "Who was it," he asked through an interpreter, "that persuaded you to lead an army into my country and so become my foe instead of remaining my friend?"

"What I did, oh, lord," Croesus responded, "has turned out to your advantage and to my loss. If there is blame, it rests with the god of the Greeks, who encouraged me to begin the war. No one is so foolish as to prefer war to peace, in which, instead of sons burying their fathers, fathers bury their sons. But the gods willed it so."[50]

Cyrus ordered Croesus's chains knocked off and had a chair brought for him so they could sit and converse, as his generals Oebares, Harpagus, Mazares, and other Persian and Median nobles gathered around to listen.

Croesus, turning and looking out over the streets of his capital below, could see Persian soldiers running amok as they looted Sardis. "May I tell you, oh, lord, what is on my mind, or is it best I remain silent?" he asked.

"Speak your mind boldly," Cyrus urged.

"What it is, oh, lord, that those men yonder are doing so busily?"

"Plundering your city," Cyrus replied, "and carrying off your riches."

"Not my city, nor my riches," Croesus came back. "They aren't mine anymore. It's *your* wealth they're pillaging."[51]

This must have brought a smile to Cyrus's face as he perceived just how right Croesus was. Ordering the members of his court to leave them, retaining just interpreters and bodyguards, Cyrus bade Croesus tell him what he should do about the looting. In response, Croesus said that Persians were a poor people, and allowing Cyrus's men to enrich themselves in this way would only make them greedy for more. And the man who looted the most would become the greediest and would rebel against Cyrus. He recommended that Cyrus place men from his bodyguard unit—full-time soldiers intensely loyal to their king—at the gates of Sardis to relieve the departing troops of their loot, using the excuse that the booty was due to their supreme god, Bel.

Seeing the wisdom of this suggestion, Cyrus ordered that the Immortals implement it at once. He then urged Croesus to ask any gift of him that he desired. Croesus would have surprised Cyrus with his subsequent request—that Lydian messengers be sent to the oracle at Delphi, taking the chains with which he had until recently been bound, to ask Apollo, via the oracle, whether it was the god's habit to deceive his benefactors. "That is the greatest favor you can bestow on me," Croesus assured his captor. He went on to relate the various questions he'd put to the oracle in the past and the responses he'd received from the

Pythoness at Delphi—responses that had led him to go to war with Cyrus.

Herodotus says that Cyrus laughed at this, no doubt delighted that a Greek king was questioning the power of the Greek gods, and said, "This I readily grant you; and anything else you shall at any time ask of me."

Croesus subsequently chose several emissaries from among his former Lydian court, men who would travel to Delphi with Cyrus's consent and there lay Croesus's chains at the temple door. Then, pointing to those chains, they were to relay a question from Croesus to Apollo, via his priests: "Aren't you ashamed for having encouraged me, as the destined destroyer of the empire of Cyrus, to begin a war with Persia, of which these were the first-fruits?" They were to then ask, "Is it the habit of the Greek gods to be ungrateful?"[52]

It would be some months before those emissaries returned, after going to the head of the line at Delphi and asking Croesus's questions. Once they did return, Croesus and Cyrus would be enlightened with epic answers that have gone down in history. First responding that Croesus's destiny had been fulfilled, the oracle went on to say that Apollo had succeeded in convincing the Fates to delay Croesus's downfall by three years, but in the end, it had been Croesus who had sealed his own fate by misinterpreting what the oracle had told him.

Because, all that the oracle had predicted had come to pass. A mule had indeed become king of Media—just as a mule is the progeny of a female horse and a male donkey, Cyrus's mother was a Mede and his father a Persian. Cyrus was the mule. As for a great empire being destroyed once Croesus crossed the Halys and went to war with Cyrus, that also had proven true—Croesus's Lydian empire had been destroyed.

Cyrus and the largest part of his army wintered at Sardis, and it was there, probably in the spring of 546 BC, that Croesus received the response from Delphi. Cyrus, deeply impressed with Croesus, decided to not only keep him close, he added him to his royal party and made him one of his counselors.

Xenophon says that Adousius had soon returned to Sardis from his mission to Caria. There Adousius had succeeded in talking his way into Halicarnassus by promising to conciliate between the city's two factions. Once inside the city, he and his troops had taken charge. He'd been able to leave a Persian garrison in the city, and Caria would become the new Persian *satrapy* of Karka. Cyrus now sent Adousius and his remaining troops to support Hystaspes on his campaign in Phrygia.

By the spring of 546 BC, an envoy from Sparta named Lacrines arrived at Sardis and sought an interview with Cyrus. King Croesus's urgent request for military aid had reached the Spartans just as they were locked in a war with the city of Argos on the Greek mainland. That conflict had resulted in a bloody Spartan victory but had prevented the Spartans from sending Croesus any troops. In any event, the swift resolution of the siege of Sardis meant that they would have arrived too late to save him. Most of the Ionian cities and the island states of the Aegean had also sought Spartan support against Cyrus, so the Spartans had sent a ship to patrol the Ionian coast for intelligence of Persian military movements, with Lacrines dispatched to Sardis with a message for Cyrus.

"In the name of the Lacedaemonians [Spartans]," Lacrines haughtily declared once his request for an audience with Cyrus was granted, "I warn you not to offer molestation to any Ionian city of Greece, as we will not allow it."

Cyrus's face clouded over once this statement had been translated for him. "Who are these Lacedaemonians?" he demanded, looking at Croesus and other Greek-speakers standing close to his throne. "And what are their number, that they dare send me such a notice?" Once the Greek-speakers had told him something of the

Spartans, Cyrus turned to Lacrines. "I have never yet been afraid of any men," he declared. "As long as I live, the Spartans will have troubles enough of their own to occupy them without concerning themselves with the Ionians!" Lacrines was sent back to Sparta with this message.[53]

Shortly after, Cyrus and Croesus set off for Ecbatana in Media. Before departing, Cyrus appointed a Persian noble, Tabalus, to the post of governor of Sardis. According to Xenophon, when Cyrus and Croesus departed, they were accompanied by a long baggage train carrying the contents of Croesus's treasuries. Xenophon claims that Croesus gave Cyrus detailed manifests of all his treasures; he may have done so, but we know that the bulk of the Lydian treasury contents actually remained in Sardis for the time being. Cyrus instructed a Lydian official named Pactyes—referred to as Pactyas by Herodotus—to collect Croesus's wealth in gold, silver, gems, jewelry, ornaments, statues, and furniture, for transportation to the Persian treasury in Anshan.

While Cyrus was on the road to Ecbatana, a courier overtook him with the news that Pactyes, the Lydian treasury official, had gone to the Ionian coast and recruited thousands of Ionian Greek mercenaries with the promise of a share of the treasuries of Croesus, adding a number of Ionian volunteers to their ranks. Then, with this force, Pactyes had surrounded and laid siege to Governor Tabalus and his Persian garrison at the citadel of Sardis. On hearing this, with his patience with the Lydians almost at an end, Cyrus spoke with Croesus.

"Where do you think this will all end, Croesus?" he said with exasperation. The Lydians, it seemed to him, were born troublemakers, and he wondered aloud if he had made a mistake in not making slaves of them all.

Croesus, hoping to save his countrymen from slavery, took advantage of the opportunity to counsel Cyrus by suggesting that the rebel official Pactyes suffer the supreme penalty for his revolt, while the remaining people of Lydia be forthwith forbidden from ever carrying arms and allowed to only wear simple clothing. Plus, he suggested that the men of Lydia only be raised to play the zither and harp or become shopkeepers and prevented from learning the military arts.

"You will soon see them become women instead of men, and there will be no more fear of them revolting from you," Croesus assured Cyrus.[54]

This advice pleased Cyrus. Summoning his Median general Mazares, he ordered him to take part of the Persian army and return to Sardis. Once Mazares had relieved the siege, he was to disarm all Lydians and issue a decree in line with Croesus's recommendations. As for anyone who had joined the Lydians in the revolt of Pactyes, if taken alive they were to be sold into slavery. Above all else, Mazares was to take Pactyes alive and bring him to Cyrus. Interestingly, it was Mazares, not Harpagus, who was entrusted with this mission. Despite coming up with his successful camel strategy for the Battle of Sardis, Harpagus had yet to gain Cyrus's full confidence.

As Cyrus continued on his way to Ecbatana, Mazares took a large detachment of troops and marched back to Sardis. When Pactyes heard that a Persian force was approaching, he panicked and fled to the coast. His leaderless army quickly dissolved, enabling Mazares to enter Sardis without meeting any resistance. Mazares immediately set in motion Cyrus's orders, and on hearing that Pactyes had been given sanctuary in the coastal city of Cyme, sent messengers demanding that he be handed over.

The people of Cyme twice consulted an oracle near Miletus to determine what they should do, and twice were told to hand Pactyes over to the Persians. Rather than surrender him, they sent him to the city of Mytilene on Lesbos. So Mazares commenced negotiations with Mytilene and was close to closing a deal whereby Mytilene was paid handsomely for handing over Pactyes, when a complication arose.

When the people of Cyme heard of Mytilene's negotiations with the Median general, they arranged for a boat that spirited Pactyes across the Aegean to Chios, fifth largest of the Greek islands, which lies just five miles off the Anatolian coast. However, the people of Chios dragged the fugitive from a temple of Minerva, where he was claiming sanctuary, and handed him over to Mazares's agents in return for rights to land on the mainland coast—once the Persians conquered it. Pactyes was sent under guard to Cyrus in Persia, and we never hear of him again.

Mazares now proceeded to march against those Ionian cities that had provided men to Pactyes for the attack on Tabalus and his Persian garrison at Sardis. He began by assaulting and taking the city of Priene, after which he sold all the inhabitants into slavery. He followed this by overrunning the entire plain watered by the Meander River and the district of Magnesia. As he paused to allow his Persian army to pillage these districts, Mazares fell ill and soon died.

When word reached Cyrus at Ecbatana that Mazares was dead, he finally gave Harpagus an independent command. Six years after Harpagus had defected to Cyrus at Pasargadae, he was dispatched to the Ionian coast to take over Mazares's army and resume the campaign against the Greek cities that had defied Cyrus. With Tabalus still in charge at Sardis, Harpagus duly commenced his Ionian campaign by besieging the port city of Phocaea.

Harpagus employed engineering against the Phocaeans, having his men use the earth they dug in creating their entrenchments to build a massive mound against the city wall. Xenophon describes siege towers on wheels Cyrus's troops employeded, and Harpagus appears to have pioneered their use. The towers were rolled up the mound to the wall, allowing Persian troops to pour over the wall and take the city. He then moved on to the next city and repeated the tactic. In this way, Harpagus was to take every Ionian Greek city in Asia Minor. But with each siege sometimes lasting months, and there being a dozen cities in the Ionian league, the task would take four years. Harpagus would not complete this mission until 542 BC.

In the meantime, Cyrus focused on creating a new Persian capital for his empire. Leaving Oebares in charge at Ecbatana, and still keeping Croesus with him, he traveled to the Persian highlands. Cyrus had decided to build his ceremonial capital at Pasargadae, center of his ancestral homeland and site of his life-changing victory over Astyages that had led to the Persians gaining their freedom from the Medes. The city would grow around a central square, Freedom Square, onto which faced a royal palace and public buildings, which were richly decorated with wall paintings. Traders and hawkers would be banned from Freedom Square. Meanwhile, Ecbatana would remain Cyrus's administrative center and home to the imperial archives.

The first work on the city of Pasargadae began in 546 BC, when part of the Persian army was occupied in the early stages of the taking of the Ionian cities. At some point during this period, Cyrus sent an instruction to Oebares in Ecbatana, telling him to have his grandfather Astyages brought to him from Barcania—according to Ctesias, Cyrus's demanding second wife, Amytis, longed to see her father.

Oebares duly sent the administration's chief eunuch Petisacas to collect Astyages. But Oebares was far from happy with his master Cyrus surrounding himself with kings he'd deposed. Apparently seeing Astyages as a threat to stable rule, Oebares instructed Petisacas to abandon Astyages in some desolate place once he had collected him, and leave him to starve to death. According to Ctesias, this is precisely what Petisacas did, and the elderly Astyages perished.

When Cyrus heard of this, he commanded Petisacas to go back, find the old king's body, and bring it to him for a proper burial, which Petisacas did. But Astyages's daughter Amytis made repeated demands for the eunuch to be punished. Yet Petisacas had only been obeying orders, and if he was indeed the same eunuch who'd convinced Astyages to let Cyrus see his parents in 552 BC, then Cyrus would have felt indebted to him for starting him down the road to power. Finally, Cyrus gave into his wife's unrelenting pressure and had Petisacas handed over to her. Amytis had Petisacas's eyes gouged out, then had him lashed until the skin hung off his back. He was then crucified. Bagapates now rose in the hierarchy to become chief eunuch in Petisacas's place.

Meanwhile, Oebares became fearful he would meet a similar, painful fate as Petisacas, even though Cyrus assured him he would allow no such thing to happen. But Cyrus had given in to nagging Amytis's demands over Petisacas, and Oebares worried that he would give in to her again. So Oebares chose to share the fate he had ordered for Astyages, starving himself to death. He took ten days to die.

This would have been an immense blow to Cyrus. He and Oebares had been through thick and thin together since before the revolution. They had fought side by side to defeat the Medians and the Lydians in often desperate battles and had been more like brothers than ruler and subject. No one would take Oebares's place as Cyrus's right-hand man. No one would rise to equal his power under Cyrus. Following these enforced deaths of his favorites Petisacas and Oebares, Cyrus seems to have tired of Amytis. She had pushed her influence too far. The couple had just one child. Cyrus's first wife, Cassandana, mother of four of his five children, seems to have come back into the picture.

When Cyrus had marched away from Lydia, leaving his generals to subdue resistance there and take the Ionian cities, "larger designs were in his mind," according to Herodotus. Once his army was free to embark on major new conquests, Cyrus was planning to personally lead his massed forces in subduing the Bactrians and the troublesome Sacae. And he was planning to invade the two major powers of the Middle East—Egypt and Babylonia.

15

FEET OF CLAY

THE BABYLONIA OF THIS TIME, or the Neo-Babylonian Empire as modern historians have labeled it, was centered on the city of Babylon, which sat astride the Euphrates River. The Iraqi city of Baghdad would much later be founded fifty-nine miles to its northwest. Babylon itself was the largest city in the Middle East and today is the largest archaeological site in the region, covering more than two thousand acres. Beyond his capital, the King of Babylon's power extended to nearby Babylonian cities such as Opis, Sippar, and Borsippa; east to Susa in the province of Elam; north to Assyria and the cities of Nineveh, Akkad, Ur, and Harran; west taking in Syria and its ancient cities of Damascus, Palmyra, and Aleppo; Phoenicia with its Mediterranean ports of Sidon and Tyre; and south to Judah and Palestine, with the Arab-controlled Negev Desert providing a border buffer zone with Egypt to the south.

King Nebuchadnezzar II, the Babylonian king who had twice conquered the kingdom of Judah, reigned for some forty-three years. Through much of this period, the Jewish exiles from Judah had made lives for themselves in Babylonia. According to the Old Testament, one of these exiles, named Nehemiah, was living with his family at Susa, called Shushan in the Bible. Others resided in various parts of Babylonia as well as at Babylon itself. The prophet Ezekiel is believed to have been settled near Nippur in the district of Sumer, where he prospered. We learn from several books of the Old Testament about the lives these exiles led.

While the book of Daniel purports to be a firsthand account by a Jewish exile in Babylonia, the consensus among many scholars and historians is that it is a work of fiction, written around 170 BC (see Afterword), to offer lessons to the Jewish faithful. For one thing, we know that some of the historical detail is incorrect. Daniel has provided some of the most colorful and memorable Bible stories: the powerful figure with feet of clay, the story of the writing on the wall, and the story of Daniel in the lions' den, all designed to give believers strength in times of trial, and set in the time of Cyrus.

However, even if Daniel is a novella containing entertaining and instructive fiction, some of the detail in it offers a picture of life under the Babylonian kings and subsequently under Cyrus that may have had an historical basis via accounts handed down through the generations. The author/s of Daniel was/were without a doubt familiar with Babylon, with sources likely to have been residents of the city as part of the Babylonian Diaspora. One or more of those sources are likely to have also visited the governor's palace at Susa in Elam Province, as well as the Karkheh River (the biblical Ulai) outside Susa, and the Tigris (Hiddekel) River, all of which are mentioned in the book of Daniel. In addition, the author/s of Daniel tell of how Nebuchadnezzar II and his successors incorporated the Jewish captives into the service of the Babylonian court.

Daniel, if you remember, was said to be one of four Jewish youths, childhood friends, who were among the several thousand Jews exiled to Babylonia after the conquest of Jerusalem. Daniel's colleagues were Hananiah, Mishael, and Azariah. The story goes that they were chosen by Ashpenaz, Nebuchadnezzar's *rab-saris*, or chief eunuch, because they were fine physical specimens and intelligent. Ashpenaz gave the boys the Babylonian names Belteshazzar, Shadrach, Meshach, and Abednego—names made particularly famous in modern times by the 1930s song "Shadrack," which was made into a hit by Louis Armstrong.

According to Daniel, this quartet went through a three-year training period at Babylon under the palace eunuch Melzar. During this time, the young Jews were forced to learn the Akkadian language of the Babylonians and were inducted into Babylonian customs, before entering the imperial civil service. They privately retained their Hebrew language and the Jewish faith and customs, and Daniel, we are told, prayed three times a day at a window facing toward Jerusalem and the destroyed Temple of Solomon. These four captives weren't alone, with a number of Jews being similarly impressed into Babylonian government service. It's believed some would have been castrated and made eunuchs— quite a price to pay for being elevated to the senior ranks of the Babylonian civil service.

Daniel was to find favor with Nebuchadnezzar—brother-in-law of King Croesus of Lydia after marrying Croesus's sister—because the young Jew showed a gift for divining dreams. This was a gift that, according to Daniel, made him ten times better at deciphering dreams than any of the magi of the Babylonian court. When still just two years into his training, he cemented this reputation by divining a dream of Nebuchadnezzar's, a dream which had defied all others. Nebuchadnezzar sent Arioch, captain of his bodyguard, to arrest and execute all diviners after not one of them had satisfied him with an interpretation of his latest dream. After Daniel assured Arioch that he could solve the riddle of the king's dream, Arioch took him to the chief eunuch.

"I have found a man of the captives of Judah that will make known to the king the interpretation," said the captain of the guard.[55]

As Arioch had no doubt informed Daniel, Nebuchadnezzar had dreamt of a giant figure standing before him. That figure's head was of the finest gold. His chest and arms were silver, his belly and thighs brass, his legs made of iron, his feet part iron and clay. And as the king watched, a massive stone appeared and smashed to pieces the figure's clay feet. The figure was toppled and destroyed, with its remnants blown away on the wind. In its place, the stone that had shattered the figure grew to occupy the world.

Daniel was brought before Nebuchadnezzar. The king was by this time in his fifties or sixties, and as shown on engravings from his reign, was clean-shaven, as indeed all Babylonians may have been in contrast with the heavily bearded Greeks, Medes, Persians, and Jews. Daniel told the king that the figure's golden head represented Nebuchadnezzar, and the other lower sections of its body represented three kings of Babylon who would come after him, while the stone represented a kingdom that would follow, a kingdom that would reign forever.

This interpretation roughly predicted the fate of the Neo-Babylonian Empire. Written centuries after the events, we believe, this tale in Daniel had the benefit of hindsight, although even then it was not historically accurate—four kings followed Nebuchadnezzar, not three. Still, the reign of the third king, Labashi-Marduk, was easy to overlook; it lasted just nine months before King Labashi-Marduk was assassinated in a coup led by Nabonidus and his son Belshazzar in 556 BC, after which Nabonidus became king.

Nebuchadnezzar supposedly saw Daniel's interpretation as presaging a golden rule for himself, with no subsequent ruler equaling him for wealth or splendor. Jewish readers would see the interpretation as forecasting the coming kingdom of God— in the form of the mighty stone encompassing the earth. This is emphasized in the book of Daniel with Nebuchadnezzar bowing down to Daniel and hailing Daniel's God of the Jews as the most powerful heavenly entity—an illusion that is quickly shattered when Daniel describes Nebuchadnezzar then ordering the worship of a new idol of his creation, based on the figure in his dream. Meanwhile, later historians would see Nebuchadnezzar's dream predicting the end of the kings of Babylon and the rise of the Persian Empire, indicating that the book of Daniel was written after the Persian occupation of Babylon.

Daniel found such royal favor because of his dream interpretation, it says in the book of Daniel, that the king elevated him to one of the top positions in his civil administration. Specifically, he appointed Daniel governor of the home province of Babylon, the most senior of all his gubernatorial posts. The governor of Babylon had for his official residence the "gate palace," a palace attached to one of Babylon's gates. This was possibly the Ishtar Gate, the largest of the inner gates on the northern side of Babylon, erected by Nebuchadnezzar in honor of the goddess Ishtar. This gate stood beside the royal palace, straddling the broad Processional Way, used in the annual Festival of Marduk, which celebrated the Babylonian New Year. Alternatively, the provincial governor's palace may have been the one that archaeologists have identified at the northern extremity of Babylon's outer wall. According to Daniel, too, the king allowed Daniel's three Jewish friends to join his gubernatorial staff.

There is no historical evidence of a Belteshazzar—Daniel's Babylonian name, which relates to Bel, the Babylonian supreme god— holding a post in Nebuchadnezzar's administration, nor for that matter of any Jew reaching the highest levels in his civil service. If the individual on whom the character of Daniel may have been based did exist, he is likely to have suffered castration to attain such a high post. We certainly hear nothing about any children of Daniel. The only indication of Daniel having family members at

Babylon comes toward the end of the text, when we are told he was in deep mourning for three weeks, possibly following the death of a parent.

There is a marked similarity between the biblical story of Daniel and that of Joseph, he of the multicolored coat, who in the much earlier book of Genesis had successfully divined a dream of a pharaoh of Egypt and as his reward was appointed vizier, or prime minister, of Egypt. The basic story in Daniel could well have been inspired by the older story of Joseph.

We are told that Nebuchadnezzar agreed to a request from Daniel to spare all the dream-divining magi, a request perhaps made because Daniel didn't want the sole responsibility of divining the king's dreams. As had been shown, Nebuchadnezzar did not hesitate to order the execution of magi who displeased him, and Daniel's chances of a long life would be enhanced if he wasn't the only interpreter of dreams. In fact, we only hear of Daniel divining one more dream for the king.

According to Daniel, Nebuchadnezzar subsequently had the massive idol raised to replicate the figure he had seen in his dream. Built of gold, silver, brass, iron, and clay, and 60 cubits, or approximately 100 feet tall, it was erected on the plain of Dura in the province of Babylon. Archaeologists have placed this plain southeast of Babylon, where a massive pedestal for an equally massive statue has been unearthed in modern times. For the statue's inauguration, Nebuchadnezzar summoned officials, members of royalty, and priests from throughout the Babylonian Empire, requiring his subjects to worship it with music and dance.

According to Daniel, Babylonian informants came to the king and told him that Daniel's three friends Shadrach, Meshach, and Abednego were not worshipping his new idol. Brought before Nebuchadnezzar, the trio refused to worship the idol, so the king angrily ordered them bound and flung into a furnace. Yet miraculously, they survived the fire with the help of an angel, according to Daniel.

After this, Nebuchadnezzar promoted all three Jews within the administration of the province of Babylon and announced that anyone across his empire caught speaking ill of the God of the Jews was to be cut to pieces, with their houses razed and turned into dunghills. Daniel himself was not accused of failing to worship the idol; perhaps he was too great a favorite of the king for anyone to risk snitching on him. Yet, following the furnace episode, we never hear of Daniel's three friends again.

The story continues in Daniel with a chapter supposedly written primarily by Nebuchadnezzar himself, telling of again consulting Daniel for the interpretation of a dream. In this dream, a holy figure from the heavens cut down a healthy fruit tree, after which the stump of the tree was circled by a band of brass and iron. Daniel interpreted the tree as representing Nebuchadnezzar, who, he said, would leave his palace and reside in the fields, living with the animals, although his kingdom would remain secure.

According to Daniel, Nebuchadnezzar was supposedly driven out of the palace at Babylon twelve months later by his enemies and subsequently dwelled in the fields. Once in the fields, the king had a revelation: "My understanding returned to me, and I blessed the Most High," Nebuchadnezzar is said to have declared. "At the same time my reason returned to me, and for the glory of my kingdom my honor and brightness returned to me. And my counselors and my lords sought me out, and I was established in my kingdom, and excellent majesty was added to me. Now I, Nebuchadnezzar, praise and honor the king of heaven."

This first-person statement reads very much like one of the proclamations that Nebuchadnezzar, his predecessors, and his successors are known to have made, as seen on surviving inscriptions on clay cylinders, tablets, and steles. It's not impossible that the author of Daniel or his source/s saw such a proclamation displayed at Babylon or another Babylonian city and incorporated it into his own account.

To a Jewish reader of the book of Daniel, the above would have given the impression that Nebuchadnezzar had converted to Judaism and was hailing Yahweh, God of the Jews, as his own. But to Nebuchadnezzar "the most high" and "the king of heaven" was Marduk, or Bel, the Babylonians' lord of lords and principal Mesopotamian god. There is no historical evidence that to his dying day, in 562 BC when he was in his early seventies, Nebuchadnezzar continued to be anything but a devout follower of Marduk and Nebu, as were his immediate successors, several of whom had Marduk and Nebu incorporated into their names.

While there is no evidence on inscriptions of Nebuchadnezzar being driven from his palace and dwelling in the countryside as described in the book of Daniel, another Jewish text speaks of the king's son, the crown prince Amel-Marduk, leading a revolt and temporarily seizing power. According to this text, the Leviticus Rabbah, Amel-Marduk was subsequently removed from power and imprisoned by Nebuchadnezzar, who seems to have temporarily vacated Babylon in the interim. If this account is true, Amel-Marduk was released from prison on his father's death to be crowned king. His reign lasted just two years, during which time he released Jeconiah, king of Judah, and treated him as an honored member of his court along with other captured rulers.

Amel-Marduk was overthrown by his brother-in-law Neriglisar, who was succeeded on his death four years later by his son Labashi-Marduk, who after his nine-month reign, was assassinated in the coup led by Nabonidus and Belshazzar. Nabonidus became Nebuchadnezzar's fourth successor in six years when he took the throne in 556 BC. Chronologically, it's not until the reign of Nabonidus that we hear of Daniel again in the book of Daniel. It indicates that Daniel no longer held a high government position or was consulted for his skill in divining dreams in the reigns that followed Nebuchadnezzar's death.

However, according to the book of Daniel, he again gained favor in the reign of King Belshazzar, who was said to be the son of Nebuchadnezzar. We know there was no son of Nebuchadnezzar named Belshazzar who reigned after him. The author of Daniel may have confused Belshazzar with Nebuchadnezzar's son Amel-Marduk, the king who released Jeconiah and was obviously favorably disposed toward Jews. In fact, Daniel 21-22 says that the figure he identified as Belshazzar knew that his father was deposed by others but went along with it, potentially a reference to the brief deposing of Nebuchadnezzar, and replacement by Amel-Marduk.

However, most historians believe that Daniel's Belshazzar was modeled on Nabonidus's son Belshazzar, who for a period of some years, ruled at Babylon on behalf of his father, who lived in semi-retirement. Belshazzar ruled without the official title of king but with command of the Babylonian army and the powers of the sovereign and would assuredly have been addressed by his court as "king." In fact, Xenophon also refers to Belshazzar as "the king" during the later Persian assault on Babylon.

We will get to Belshazzar in the following chapters, but first it's important to discuss the reign of his father Nabonidus, who found himself at war with Cyrus. On taking the Babylonian throne, Nabonidus set out to make his mark by ordering cessation of daily worship of the principal Babylonian god Marduk. He likewise sidelined the worship of Marduk's son Nabu. This was even though Nabonidus was personally named for Nabu. Instead, Nabonidus required that the moon god Sin—pronounced Su'en—be worshipped as principal god across the Babylonian Empire. This act was influenced by Nabonidus's mother Addagoppe, also known as Adad-Guppi, who was a priestess of Sin at her birthplace, the city of Harran in northern Assyria, traditionally the center of Sin worship. A stele found in Harran tells us that Addagoppe had dreamt that her son Nabonidus would restore the temple of Sin at Harran, and all the city of Harran.

We know that Nabonidus called together the magi from throughout the Babylonian Empire for an assembly at the Esagila, the seven-story Temple of Marduk structure erected at the center of Babylon a century earlier by the Assyrians. "He assembled the priestly scholars," says an engraved text from Nabonidus's reign. At this assembly, he informed the magi that he was making a drastic change to their religion.[56]

"I am wise," he declared. "I know. I have seen what is hidden. I have seen secret things. The god Ilteri [another name for moon god Sin] has made me see a vision, has shown me everything. I am aware of a wisdom which greatly surpasses even that of the series of insights which Adapa has composed." Adapa was a character from Mesopotamian mythology; the first man created by the gods, he was the Babylonian Adam. Adapa was considered especially wise, even though he'd declined the godly gift of immortality.

Standing before the assembled priestly scholars, Nabonidus pointed to "representations" engraved on the wall of the Esagila. "He looks at the representations and utters blasphemies," the priests of Marduk would disdainfully record, and "showed them a symbol—he said it was actually of Sin, not of Marduk." Sin was represented by the symbols of a crescent moon and a wild bull called the aurochs, a now extinct cattle breed with large horns that was common in Mesopotamia.[57]

Nabonidus ordered that the Temple of Marduk at Babylon no longer receive daily offerings and canceled the annual Festival of Marduk, which involved "the most important ritual observances" on the Babylonian calendar up to that time.[58] Later events suggest that Nabonidus had the doors to the Esagila removed. The priests of Marduk continued to maintain the Babylonian calendar and royal records of Nabonidus, but their influence with the crown was now next to nothing.

Then Nabonidus promptly embarked on the total restoration of the Elhulhul, or House of Joy, the rundown temple of Sin in

Harran—a city believed by many historians to have not only been his mother's hometown but also Nabonidus's birthplace. He would boast that he used cedars of Lebanon for the doors of the Elhulhul and for its thousands of new roof timbers, that he adorned the gates with gold and silver, and "made its walls shine like the sun." Inside, he erected a massive statue of Sin on an equally massive pedestal. "He made an image of a deity which nobody has ever seen in this country," the priests of Marduk would complain. The god's long hair fell all the way down to the pedestal, while around his neck was draped a lapis lazuli necklace. On his head, the god wore a tiara. Out the front of the temple, Nabonidus erected massive silver alloy statues of aurochs.[59]

Once the Elhulhul restoration was complete—the work seems to have lasted two to three years—Nabonidus led a procession from Babylon to Harran to inaugurate the new temple, a journey that would have taken weeks. That procession had been part of his mother's dream and involved statues of Sin, Sin's wife Ningal, Nusku the god of light and fire, and Nusku's wife Sadarnunna. In Harran, Nabonidus's mother would have proudly welcomed the procession, with her son at its head. She would live to a great age, dying in 544 BC at the claimed age of 104. Just as his mother's dream had also required, Nabonidus enriched the entire city of Harran with new decoration. He was to boast: "I made the city of Harran, in its totality, as brilliant as moonlight."[60]

During this period, too, Nabonidus restored two temples at the city of Sippar, fifty miles north of Babylon, and he probably inaugurated them en route to Harran. One was the temple of Samas (Shamash), son of Sin, Babylonian judge of heaven and the underworld. Nebuchadnezzar had previously restored this temple, but forty-five years later, its walls were sagging and crying out for remedial attention. Nabonidus undertook a total rebuild, which included five thousand new cedar roof beams.

The second temple to be restored by Nabonidus at Sippar was

that of Anunitu. This deity, originally worshipped as an Assyrian goddess of childbirth, later became one of the facets of the goddess Inanna, better known as Ishtar, goddess of war. She was the daughter of Sin. In her martial guise, she was always depicted armed, and at the Sippar temple Nabonidus had her shown with bow and quiver. We know from archaeological discoveries that in his reign Nabonidus also dedicated a temple of Sin at Ur and a temple of Samas at Larsa.

He had originally promised that, once all these temples had been opened, he would restore the Festival of Marduk. But he failed to keep his word, and the festival remained off the calendar. Late in the third year of his reign, once he had implemented his religious reforms, Nabonidus considered his work done. While he himself retained the title and dignity of king, he appointed his son Belshazzar commander in chief of his armies and installed him at Babylon to administer his empire. Nabonidus then took part of the army and marched southwest to the desert oasis city of Tema, or Tayma as it is known today.

This city, sitting in the north of today's Kingdom of Saudi Arabia, was on the main route from Babylon to Egypt and stood astride the caravan road from the Persian Gulf to the Gulf of Aqaba. Strategically placed, wealthy, and enjoying a mild climate, Tema was then controlled by a local Arab prince. Nabonidus's army soon dealt with the prince's small army and terminated the prince, although it seems some of Nabonidus's nobles perished in the fighting while he watched on—the Verse Account of Nabonidus refers to his nobles dying in war.

Nabonidus then set about turning Tema into his private retirement center. Enslaving the city's entire native population, he set them all, men, women, and children, to work slaving on major construction projects. He had a palace built in Tema that was a replica of his palace at Babylon. And he had a massive brick wall built around the city—archaeologists have unearthed remains of its three-mile circuit—placing troops of his bodyguard in forts around the perimeter. He then settled down to idle away the rest of his days in luxurious retirement while he allowed his son to run roughshod over the Babylonian people in his name.

The Verse Account of Nabonidus, written during and just after his reign, complains: "Law and order aren't promulgated by him. He made the common people perish through want, the nobles he killed in war, for the trader he blocked the road. He took away their property, scattered possessions." Everywhere, Babylonians wore grim faces. "You don't see happiness anymore," moaned the priests of Marduk.

Within ten years, Nabonidus's retirement was to be rudely interrupted by a military threat—not via an uprising by his own dissatisfied subjects, but by Cyrus and the Persian army.

16

MARCHING ON BABYLON

Y 542 BC, Cyrus had completed the conquest of all the
nations and cities of mainland Asia Minor—the Greek island
states remained unconquered, and opposed to Cyrus, but were too
small to individually pose a threat to him. Herodotus says that
while Harpagus led one Persian army in the south, mostly along
the Aegean coast, Cyrus had personally led another in conquering
Assyria to the north—up till then a Babylonian possession.

We know that at some point during this period, Cyrus also conquered Urartu, the Armenian highlands Kingdom of Van, called
Ararat in the Bible, which was centered around Lake Van. Previously
a Median possession, Van seems to have attempted to assert its independence once Cyrus deposed Astyages. According to another Babylonian text, the Nabonidus Chronicle, Cyrus killed a king during
one of his campaigns in the 540s BC, and historians believe this was
the king of Van, who probably fell in battle against Cyrus. Following
Van's defeat, Cyrus turned it into the Persian satrapy of Armenia.

Along the Aegean coast of Anatolia, Harpagus was faced with a
grinding campaign against the Ionian and Aeolian Greek city-states.

This often involved lengthy sieges, which were usually terminated with the aid of Harpagus's trademark earth mounds as well as several pitched battles in the open. As Harpagus defeated each city, its surviving fighting-age men were drafted into his army, increasing its size. Two of the battles saw Harpagus's vastly larger army wipe out the opposition. The city of Xanthus lost every citizen other than eighty families who were living elsewhere at the time. With their city walls surrounded, the Xanthian men packed their wives, children, and slaves onto their acropolis at the center of the city and burned them all to death, adding their treasure to the fire. The men then surged from Xanthus to make a suicidal charge at the Persians, a charge in which every one of them perished.

The Persian conquest was made all the more difficult by cities in Caria that had previously submitted to Mazares rejoining the resistance behind Harpagus's back. The people of the inland Carian city of Pedasia fled to a mountain and built fortifications there. Herodotus says they gave Harpagus enormous trouble and stubbornly held out, perhaps for years, before finally succumbing to the relentless Persian campaign. Meanwhile, other cities such as Cnidus in Caria surrendered before the Persians even launched a siege.

With the Ionian and Aeolian cities of Asia Minor in his hands, along with Cilicia, Cappadocia, Lycia, Lydia, and Assyria, Cyrus turned his eyes to Elam. He would have long wanted to free the people of Elam, neighbors of Persis who had a similar ethnic background to the Persians. Elam, with its capital at the historic city of Susa, lay east of Babylon. With Elam under his control, Cyrus could address Babylon itself.

Cyrus knew that Babylonia was ripe for invasion. With King Nabonidus semi-retired in Tema and his son Belshazzar living the high life at Babylon, there was much discontent throughout the Babylonian Empire. Development of the city of Babylon under a plan Nebuchadnezzar had initiated had stopped, with the work incomplete. The welfare of the common people had been neglected under Nabonidus, and the priests who had previously been at the center of their lives, the magi of Marduk, had been sidelined.

Most importantly, for ten years during the reign of Nabonidus the New Year Festival of Marduk, which traditionally took place following the spring equinox of March 21, officially the start of the new year in Mesopotamia, had been erased from the calendar. Traditionally, the festival, which continues to be celebrated to this day in Iran as *Nowruz* and lasts thirteen days, had begun with the statue of Nabu, son of Marduk, being carried to the capital from the Ezida, the temple of Nabu complex at the lakeside city of Borsippa eleven miles downstream from Babylon. The Ezida temple of Nabu and Babylon's Esagila Temple of Marduk were identical 220-foot high, seven-level ziggurats, with bricks covered in a shining rich blue glaze of lapis lazuli.

Once Nabu arrived outside Babylon, Marduk "came out" to meet his son, with his statue carried from his temple in the Esagila, then out the Ishtar Gate and down the broad Processional Way, which ran from south to north through the center of the city's eastern district and then out into the suburbs. The Processional Way was spectacularly paved with colored stone and lined with huge statues of lions. At a holy place outside the city walls, the two statues were united and then paraded around amid singing and dancing.

The Festival of Marduk had been the source of great joy to the people. It was an event, like modern New Year celebrations, that they looked forward to from year to year. For religious Babylonians, it was as if they had been cut off from their god. It would have had the same impact on believers as would the erasure of the Christian Easter or the Muslim Ramadan today. The priests of Marduk at Babylon sadly recorded that, at the usual time when each annual New Year festival should have been celebrated for a decade during the reign of Nabonidus, "Marduk did not come out."[61]

Cyrus was very much aware of this. He would go down on record professing a firm reverence for Marduk and Nabu, and he could also see how he could exploit the feelings of Nabonidus's Babylonian subjects and win their loyalty by restoring the worship of Marduk and Nabu at Babylon. When, in 540 BC, he sent a Persian army into Elam, he would have instructed the spies whom Xenophon says he always employed ahead of military campaigns to spread the word throughout Babylonia that he intended to restore Marduk to his proper place at Babylon.

Susa soon fell to Cyrus's troops, apparently without a pitched battle or lengthy siege. The Elamites probably rose up against their Babylonian overlords as the Persian army approached. From this point on, Cyrus allowed Elamites to become members of his Immortals bodyguard, alongside Persians and Medians. He would also make Susa one of the principal cities of the Persian Empire. According to Xenophon, Cyrus would in the future always spend the spring in Susa. And he would establish the Persian Royal Road linking Susa to Sardis in Lydia. With Elam under his control, Cyrus was able to seal off Babylonia's eastern border. Now, he could focus on taking Babylon itself.

Even in retirement, Nabonidus had, for years, been very much aware of the threat Cyrus posed. After Cyrus defeated Astyages and conquered Media, the priests of Marduk had recorded Nabonidus as saying, "I became troubled. I was worried, and my face showed signs of anxiety."[62] This was magian propaganda, but it reflected the fact that Nabonidus was nervous of Cyrus's intentions. The fall of Lydia to Cyrus and then the Persian conquest of all of Asia Minor would have troubled him even more. Yet, Nabonidus didn't have the courage to confront Cyrus as he took Assyria from him, even when his holy birthplace of Harran fell to the Persians. Nabonidus could have marched a massive Babylonian army north to do battle with Cyrus, but he didn't.

Instead, Nabonidus had statues of Babylonian gods removed from their temples in threatened cites east of the Tigris and brought to Babylon. Then, he tried to bluff Babylonians into believing he

had dealt with the Persians, issuing an outrageously false proclamation about Cyrus which was distributed on clay tablets: "I
have made him bow to my feet. I personally have conquered his
countries, his possessions I took to my residence." Clearly, he was
trying to explain away the arrival over several months of his own
gold and silver statuary by the caravan-load in Babylon as Cyrus's
possessions.[63]

Up until the loss of Elam, Nabonidus had been in denial. The
fall of Susa jerked him into action. Over the winter of 540/539 BC,
he returned to Babylon from Tema and took back control of the
Babylonian armed forces from Belshazzar. And very much aware
of how unhappy his subjects were about the banning of the Festival of Marduk for the past decade, he proclaimed that the festival
would again take place that year. Sure enough, the Festival of Marduk was celebrated to welcome in the new year at the commencement of the spring of 539 BC. But, had Nabonidus acted too late to
save his crown?

In the summer of 539 BC, Cyrus's army moved inexorably south.
Cyrus was in sole command. He had appointed his top general
Harpagus satrap for all Asia Minor following its conquest, based
in Lycia. Perhaps the four years of hard campaigning had affected
Harpagus's health. Certainly the continued presence of his able,
pragmatic, and now trusted Mede general in Asia Minor assured
Cyrus that he could focus on Babylonia while Harpagus kept the
newly conquered territories to his back under firm control.

The presence of King Croesus in Cyrus's party for the Babylonian campaign is not recorded, although he would accompany
Cyrus on a later campaign. Hystaspes, father of Darius and satrap
of Persis, is not mentioned either, although he would also later
campaign with Cyrus. According to Xenophon, a eunuch named
Gadatas was now in Cyrus's party. Holding a senior post in the
Babylonian king's service, he'd defected to Cyrus. The third or
second century BC Jewish Book of Tobit mentions a Babylonian

official named Gadatas during the later reign of Darius. We also know, from a letter by Darius, of a Greek-speaking administrator in coastal Asia Minor named Gadatas during his reign, and this is likely to have been the same man.

Cyrus's eldest son, Cambyses, was also in his party. Now aged twenty, Cambyses was being groomed as his father's successor. As a child, he had suffered from seizures, which Herodotus describes as the result of "the sacred sickness," as the ancients called epilepsy. Cambyses seems to also have had eye problems, for Cyrus sent a request to the Pharaoh of Egypt, Amasis, for the best eye doctor in his service. Wishing to keep on good terms with Cyrus, Pharaoh Amasis had sent the eye doctor to the Persian court, parting the man from his wife and children—for many years it turned out.

No classical source tells us whom Cyrus wished the doctor to treat, but there is no mention of Cyrus himself suffering eye problems, and we know that this very doctor remained on the staff of his son Cambyses following Cyrus's death. Almost certainly the eye doctor's patient was Cambyses, meaning that he suffered from vision problems as well as epileptic seizures, symptoms which point to a cause that will be discussed in a later chapter. There is no record of Cambyses becoming involved in the fighting during this campaign—later, when Darius the Great was twenty, he was considered to have not yet reached Persian military service age, and this is likely to also have applied to Cambyses. Instead, Cambyses watched and learned from his father's side.

As the Persian army marched down the east bank of the Tigris River, north of Opis, it came to a rushing, roaring river called the Gyndes, a tributary of the Tigris known today as the Diyala. This river blocked Cyrus's path and halted the advance. Herodotus says that, as Cyrus considered how he could best cross the Gyndes, one of the sacred white horses in his column broke loose and attempted to swim the river. The icy, fast-flowing waters from the

Zagros Mountains knocked the horse from its feet and swept it away, causing the horse to drown.

Herodotus says that Cyrus was so angry he vowed to punish the river, although what followed was more likely based on a sound engineering concept: he had his men dig 360 channels, 180 on each bank, to divert the course of the Gyndes so that men, horses, and vehicles could easily ford it. But this engineering work took weeks, and by the time it was completed, the summer had passed. The fact that a massive Persian army was toiling to the north of Opis was soon communicated to King Nabonidus at Babylon.

The delay caused by the diversion of the Gyndes gave Nabonidus time to assemble a large Babylonian army and march it north from Babylon. Over several days, this force followed the Euphrates fifty miles to the city of Sippar. Babylonia was in those times crisscrossed by straight canals, and King Nebuchadnezzar had built a large royal canal through productive wheat and barley fields from Sippar due east to Opis on the Tigris. On the north side of this waterway, Nebuchadnezzar used the spoil from the canal to build a defensive earth barrier. Known as the Median Wall, it was designed to keep out the Medes. Troops were posted along this wall and at Sippar and Opis at either end.

Nabonidus based himself at Sippar, putting someone else in charge of the army that encamped on the plain outside Opis to the east and prepared to do battle with the approaching Persians. The Opis commander may have been the crown prince Belshazzar, although later events suggest that Nabonidus had left him in charge at Babylon. We know that another senior Babylonian official was in the area at the time. This was the governor of Babylonia's Gutium province, which lay north of Elam and to the east of Babylon, extending beyond the Tigris toward the Zagros Mountains.

Xenophon calls this governor Gobryas and describes him as an elderly Assyrian. However, Xenophon seems to have confused this figure with a Persian noble named Gobryas, who would, seventeen years after this, help bring Darius I to the Persian throne. The much more reliable Nabonidus Chronicle gives two names, Ugbara and the very similar Gubara—many scholars believe this was the one and the same man, and was Xenophon's Gobryas. Gubara, the governor of Gutium, may have commanded at Opis.

In the last days of September, Cyrus arrived outside Opis, and the Babylonian army marched out from their camp and formed up for combat. We have no details of the Battle of Opis. Both armies would have been large, but Cyrus's army, made up of Persians, Medes, Elamites, and men from the newly conquered cities of Asia Minor, all marching under their national banners, would have been massive. Xenophon puts Cyrus's cavalry arm alone by this time at 40,000 men. An additional 150,000 spearmen, archers, and slingers is not unlikely. What a difference from the force of the few thousand Persian rebels Cyrus had led into battle on Persian soil a decade earlier. Now Cyrus led a multinational force based around a highly disciplined, well trained, and intensely dedicated Persian and Median core. Now Cyrus led a war machine.

Cyrus's standard, the red and gold *Shahbaz*, was raised. The lines of troops faced off. Cyrus gave the order for the charge. As men dashed forward, spears and arrows filled the air. Xenophon says that Cyrus had trained his troops to always quickly advance and engage in close combat with sword and battle-ax, rather than stand back and exchange stones, arrows, and spears as had been custom for the armies of many of his opponents. We do know that the battle was fierce, and we know that the Babylonians were bloodily defeated.

Xenophon gives an account of one of Cyrus's battles, at an unidentified location, where the opposing forces broke in panic and fled from him to entrenchments outside a nearby military camp, where many were crushed to death by their terrified colleagues and the rest massacred by their attackers. This could well have occurred outside Opis. The Nabonidus Cylinder also tells of many Babylonian troops being massacred at this point, which has led some scholars to suggest that they were killed by Nabonidus after they revolted against him. However, massacre at the gates of Opis by Cyrus's troops seems the much more likely scenario.

The city of Opis surrendered. At Sippar, King Nabonidus, on receiving the news of the loss of Opis, deserted his subjects and fled south toward Babylon. In his rush, even his statues of the children of Sin were left behind in Sippar. Almost certainly, Nabonidus and his entourage took boats down the Euphrates. The river's rapid southerly flow meant that not even cavalry could overtake them. Herodotus tells us that the cargo craft that came down the Euphrates from as far north as Armenia were round. Built on wicker frames and covered with skins, even the largest of these required a crew of just two men on steering oars; the current was so strong that the river itself provided the propulsion. Once the boats reached Babylon and were unloaded, their crewmen dismantled them and returned home by road with them.

According to the Babylonian scribe Berossus, who would some time later serve as a magus of Marduk at Babylon, Nabonidus didn't stay long at Babylon once he reached the city. Leaving Belshazzar in command at the capital, the king continued eleven miles downriver to the city of Borsippa, center of worship of Nabonidus's namesake Nabu. There in that city's royal palace, the king fearfully holed up.

Following the capture of Opis, Cyrus allowed his men to plunder the city and the dead enemy troops, then recrossed the Tigris at the ford he'd created above Opis and marched his army west beside the Median Wall across the plain to Sippar at the Euphrates. Sippar surrendered without a fight on October 6, a date stemming from a reliable contemporary inscription. It seems that it was at this point—certainly no later—that Gubara the governor came over to Cyrus's side. According to Xenophon, Gobryas (Gubara) had some time before this sent Cyrus word of his intent to defect, bringing his mounted troops with him. Cyrus was soon to entrust great responsibility to Gubara.

Cyrus immediately advanced south to Babylon with his army, following the eastern bank of the Euphrates. Possibly, he himself traveled in a chariot drawn by four sacred Persian white horses, with his baggage trains and camp-followers trailing back over the horizon. "His vast troops," says the Cyrus Cylinder, "whose number, like the waters in a river, could not be counted, were marching fully armed at his side."

For the army to be fully armed, rather than in column of march with some weapons and equipment on baggage animals and wagons, shows that Cyrus was fully prepared for the Babylonians to come out to meet him and do battle while he was on the march. But once he reached the sprawling city of Babylon, he found that his opponents were skulking behind Babylon's massive walls. All the bronze gates, including those of the huge north-facing Ishtar Gate, were firmly closed, and the walls were lined with the city's defenders.

Prince Belshazzar and the many thousands of people in the city had long prepared for a siege; Herodotus says they had accumulated enough supplies to hold out for years. From their walls, they surveyed the Persian army as it arrived on the broad river plain below, no doubt with a mixture of trepidation at the threatening sight and confidence in the impregnability of the defenses of their city, the greatest and best-fortified city in the world at that time.[64]

Overall, Babylon formed a vast triangle, with central Babylon taking a roughly rectangular shape toward the bottom of the triangle. Central Babylon was split in two by the broad Euphrates River. As the outermost line of defense, a moat was said to surround the entire city—although archaeologists have found no trace of this. However, on the Cyrus Cylinder, Cyrus tells of adding to the brick quay beside the moat. We know there were brick quays either side of the Euphrates where it ran through Babylon, and it's likely the river was considered to act as a moat on the river sides of east and west Babylon. A pair of massive walls, an inner and an outer, ran around three sides for fifteen miles in each direction. These walls were some eighty feet tall. The inner wall was so broad that single-chamber buildings sat atop it, divided by a street wide enough for a four-horse chariot to turn.

"The city was even better protected by its river than by its walls," says Xenophon. The Euphrates was at least a quarter of a mile wide when it ran through Babylon. On the riverbanks, brick fences and wooden gates separated the city streets from brick and stone quays, where in peacetime, freight from upriver was unloaded and freight bound for what we today call the Persian Gulf to the south was loaded. At the center of the city, a bridge crossed the river from east Babylon to west Babylon via a number of brick piers, with the walkway's ends drawn up, drawbridge-style, at night.

Inside the walls, the city was divided into districts, each with neat grid-pattern streets, lined with three- and four-story brick residences. The eastern portion of the two halves of Babylon was the largest and contained the most impressive and most important buildings, although there were temples in both sectors. At the heart of the eastern district, not far from the river and the bridge, stood the dominating Esagila complex, which contained two temples of Marduk. Herodotus says that inside the main temple there was a golden table and superhuman size couch, where the god was said to sleep. In a smaller temple in the north of the complex, there was a massive golden statue of a seated Marduk. Foreigners and armed men were forbidden by law to enter the walled temple complex, which in normal times was protected by dedicated temple guards known as the Shield Bearers.

The citadel of Babylon, home to the royal guard, dominated a rise near the city's northern wall in the eastern district. Next to it stood the royal palace, protected by a high wall. Just to the east of the palace was the massive and dazzling Ishtar Gate, the bricks of its gleaming blue-glazed walls decorated with motifs of the lion, aurochs, and an amphibious dragon, which the Babylonians sometimes called the Storm Dragon because in their mythology, Marduk caught it in a storm. The Ishtar Gate was considered one of the Wonders of the Ancient World.

According to Berossus, another of those Ancient Wonders, the famed Hanging Gardens of Babylon, were connected to the palace. He claimed that Nebuchadnezzar built these fabulous elevated gardens for his Median wife Amytis, to remind her of home. The problem is, none of the classical Greek authors such as Herodotus, who visited Babylon, make any mention of the Hanging Gardens, and no archaeological evidence of their existence has ever been unearthed at Babylon. Some scholars believe the Hanging Gardens were actually at Nineveh, the Assyrian capital, which was almost totally destroyed by the Babylonians when they conquered Assyria.

Xenophon says that once Cyrus arrived outside Babylon, he called a war council of his senior generals and advisers to consider how to break into the city and reach the royal palace. Herodotus confesses that he didn't know whether the strategy Cyrus now came up with was his own idea or was suggested to him. This suggestion may have come from Gubara the governor. Noted author of science fiction H.G. Wells, who wrote the bestselling 1921 nonfiction book *The Outline of History,* suggested in his book that Cyrus's plan for taking Babylon involved the connivance of the priests of Bel, the magi of Marduk, who were resident in Babylon. As will be seen, the plan didn't involve an "inside job" as such, but it certainly required in-depth knowledge of the history and layout of Babylon. Perhaps one or more of the magi did find their way to Cyrus to offer advice.

Firstly, Cyrus divided his army into two groups. One force, referred to here as North Force, was stationed on the eastern bank of the Euphrates, where the river entered the city. The other army group, South Force, he sent marching around the eastern side of Babylon to where the river emerged from the city to the south, thus covering any attempted escapes from Babylon by water. This march would have taken at least a day.

In the meantime, Cyrus took all the noncombatants in his party—thousands of slaves including personal servants and baggage-handlers—and withdrew north. He went as far as a basin, which Herodotus says a queen of Babylon named Nitocris had dug. Nitocris had done this to temporarily divert the course of the Euphrates, permitting the construction of the piers of the bridge that now spanned the river linking east and west Babylon.

Scholars are divided as to who Nitocris was. Some suggest she was the wife of a seventh century BC king. Herodotus says she was a wife of Nabonidus, and some scholars believe she was also a daughter of Nebuchadnezzar. If she was indeed Nabonidus's wife, Nitocris may have carried out her ambitious Euphrates engineering project while Nabonidus was living in Tema. Once the Babylon bridge had been completed, Nitocris had redirected the river back to its original course.

Taking a leaf from Nitocris's playbook, Cyrus set his slaves to work digging a broad channel from Nitocris's basin to the river and also had them chop down palm trees for miles around. After just several days' work, Cyrus was ready to use hundred-foot palm tree trunks to create a levy that would divert much of the flow of the Euphrates into this channel. Once the last earth was removed between the channel and the river, river waters would wash into marshland that occupied Nitocris's old basin. Prior to this, says Xenophon, the river was so deep that one man could stand on another's shoulders and still be underwater. Herodotus says that by the time Cyrus had finished, the river's depth, as it flowed through the city, dropped to the point that it only reached halfway up a man's thigh.

All this had been done out of sight of Babylon, so that the people in the city had no inkling of what was going on. It was also done to a strict timetable. That timetable was dictated by the fact that on the night of October 12, an annual religious festival was to be celebrated in the city. This festival may have been the *Mehregan*, an October festival dedicated to principal god Marduk. It became so engrained in Persian life that it is still enthusiastically celebrated in Iran today, taking place on October 2. Another suggestion is that the October 12 event was a festival of Sin, although the way the inhabitants of Babylon were to embrace the festival on this night, and the fact that Nabonidus had recently reinstated Marduk worship, seem to rule out anything connected with the "alien" god Sin.

Cyrus knew that on the night of October 12, the inhabitants of Babylon would be feasting, drinking, and dancing until dawn. With the river's diversion timed to take place after dark, no one in the city was any the wiser when the level of the river dropped. Now Cyrus, who had never visited Babylon in his life, ordered Gubara to lead a surprise commando raid that would gain entry to the city. He gave Gubara a small force of selected men who would enter and follow the now lowered Euphrates in the dark and penetrate east Babylon from the riverside. Then, using his firsthand knowledge of the city, Gubara was to make his way directly to the palace and take King Nabonidus prisoner.

For Cyrus harbored the belief that Nabonidus had retreated to the city and taken refuge at the palace—the last intelligence he'd received about Nabonidus at Sippar would have been of him fleeing south toward Babylon following the fall of Opis. Once Gubara had secured the king, he was then to open gates in the northern walls and admit a Persian cavalry force waiting outside the city.

While Cyrus remained at his camp by Nitocris's basin, in the early hours of the morning Gubara led a group of perhaps hundreds of men who silently slipped into the chilly Euphrates waters and waded for several miles along the river, whose bed, says Xenophon, now "formed a highway into the heart of the town." As Herodotus points out, had the Babylonians woken up to what was going on, they could have lined the fences on either side of the river and poured arrows and spears into the Persians, who would have been trapped like sitting ducks between them once they reached central Babylon, and the Babylonians could have "destroyed them utterly." But Marduk the patron god of Babylon would be seen to be with Cyrus. With the aid of scaling ladders, says Xenophon, the Persian troops climbed the riverbank onto the quays and then mounted the brick fences edging the quays, dropping into the city just south of the palace.

With the sounds of music, singing, dancing, and laughter still in the air from remaining revelers, and many other Babylonians lost in drunken sleep, Gubara the defector led his Persian troops unerringly along east-west and then north-south streets toward the palace entrance. Xenophon says that "those they met were struck down and slain, and some fled into their houses." Some Babylonians, he says, tried to raise the alarm, but Gubara and his men drowned out their dying cries with yells of their own, as they pretended to be drunken revelers.

The advance party, whose job it was to secure the bronze palace gates, arrived at the trot to find the gates closed. But the Babylonian guards stationed outside were drinking around a large fire. The Persian advance party leapt on the royal guards from the darkness, and a mighty struggle ensued in the firelight, as the outnumbered Babylonian guards bellowed for help from inside the palace walls.

17

THE WRITING IS ON THE WALL FOR NABONIDUS

T HAT NIGHT FOR THE FESTIVAL, Belshazzar, King Nabonidus's son and heir, held a feast for a thousand at Babylon's royal palace, in defiance of the fact that the Persian army had arrived outside the city walls. According to the book of Daniel, for this feast Belshazzar decided to use the thirty golden drinking cups that Nebuchadnezzar had looted from Jerusalem's Temple of Solomon and had them brought from the royal treasury. In separate men's and women's dining rooms, Belshazzar, his sons, wives, and concubines drank Armenian wine from these golden cups, toasting the gods of gold, silver, brass, iron, wood, and stone.

Belshazzar then noticed that someone had written something on the plastered wall, near a candlestick: "MENE MENE TEKEL UPHARSIN." These words were in Aramaic, the language of the western part of the empire, the language of the Jews. They referred to weights and measures, and meant, literally, "two minas, a shekel, and two parts." This made no sense to Belshazzar. Curious and unnerved, he called for the leading magi.

"Whoever can read this writing and show me its interpretation," said the Akkadian-speaking prince, probably drunkenly, "shall be clothed in scarlet and have a chain of gold around his neck, and shall be the third ruler in the kingdom." Scholars debate what post Belshazzar was actually offering here. It could have been, as in the later Persian administration of Babylon described in Daniel 6, the third-most senior deputy administrator in the land. Or it could have been a post that ranked third in the kingdom after his father the king and Belshazzar himself—a sort of prime minister.

According to Daniel, the magi could make neither head nor tail of this writing. Belshazzar, greatly troubled, berated his courtiers until he was red in the face, terrifying them. And then "the queen" heard the shouting and came into the king's banqueting chamber to try to calm Belshazzar—the women being required to dine separately. Many scholars take this queen to mean King Nabonidus's wife and Belshazzar's mother or stepmother, Nitocris.

"Oh, king, may you live forever," she said, using the traditional greeting to the sovereign. "There is a man in your kingdom in whom there is the spirit of the holy gods." She went on to tell him that in the days of King Nebuchadnezzar, this man had proven very wise, and Nebuchadnezzar had appointed him master of the magicians, astrologers, and soothsayers, and he had shown great ability to interpret dreams. This man was called Daniel, she said, or Belteshazzar, as he'd been renamed when he joined the court staff. "Let Daniel be called," the queen urged, "and he will give you an interpretation."[65]

So, guards were sent to fetch Daniel. Having lost the post of governor of the province of Babylon that he'd held under Nebuchadnezzar, Daniel no longer lived in the gate palace. But he would have still lived in east Babylon, for the bridge to west Babylon was raised at night—unless it was left down for the festival. The now middle-aged Daniel was duly brought into the banqueting hall, and he prostrated himself before the angry crown prince.

"Are you Daniel, one of the captive children of Judah, whom King Nebuchadnezzar brought out of Jewry?" asked Belshazzar, according to the book of Daniel. "I've heard of you." He went on to tell Daniel about the writing on the wall and the inability of the magi to decipher it. And he offered him scarlet robes, a gold neck-chain, plus the post of third ruler in the kingdom, if he could interpret the writing's message.

Daniel responded by telling Belshazzar to keep his gifts and give them to somebody else—he would gladly interpret the mysterious writing. But before he did, he boldly castigated the prince for using the gold drinking cups from the Temple of Solomon. He then proceeded to give a reading of the message on the wall. MENE, he said, meant that God had fixed the duration of the reign of Belshazzar and his father, which was about to end. TEKEL meant that Belshazzar's fate had been weighed on the scales and been found wanting. PERES meant that the kingdom of Babylonia was going to be divided among the Medes and the Persians.

In response to this, Belshazzar ordered Daniel to be clothed in scarlet and draped with a golden neck-chain, despite his protests, and had a proclamation prepared announcing that Daniel was to be the third-ranking man in the land. Now this all sounds surprising, considering the fact that Daniel had just predicted the downfall of the Babylonian monarchy and the end of Belshazzar and his father. But perhaps this interpretation accorded with Belshazzar's own feelings of foreboding, and this was why he'd sent for the golden cups from Jerusalem, being imbued with a pessimistic sentiment of "drink and be merry, for tomorrow we die." And perhaps he rewarded Daniel because he'd been the only diviner with the courage to say what most of the frightened nobility of Babylon were thinking.

Daniel was not to enjoy his new appointment. Xenophon tells us why. Noise from the life-and-death struggle outside the palace gate alarmed those inside, and word was sent to Belshazzar in the banqueting hall. He gave orders for men of his bodyguard to investigate. As soon as these men opened the gates to find out what was going on, waiting Persian commandos rushed them. According to Xenophon, scores of Persians overwhelmed many of these bodyguards. As other guards fled back inside, the defector Gadatas the eunuch, who was familiar with the palace layout, led Persian troops through the open gates toward the royal banqueting hall.

The Persian insurgents found Belshazzar, a sword in hand, accompanied by a small entourage and prepared to stand his ground and fight. Probably worse the wear from a night of drinking, the prince was felled as he battled these attackers. All those with him also died. Some stood and fought, using whatever was at hand as a shield, says Xenophon. Others tried to flee. All were cut down. Most of the thousand banquet guests had apparently fled and hidden themselves throughout the palace, offering no resistance; none loved Belshazzar or his father enough to give their lives for them. Daniel, the new prime minister, must have been among those skulking in the palace, for according to the book of Daniel, he survived this deadly night.

Persian troops quickly secured the palace. The adjacent Ishtar Gate was apparently then opened from the inside, followed by an outer gate, for Xenophon says that Persian cavalry entered the city and ranged the streets, killing anyone they found. Men among the troopers who spoke the Akkadian tongue of the Babylonians yelled a warning to the population to stay indoors, under pain of death if they disobeyed. Herodotus says that much of the population of the city remained totally unaware that the Persians had occupied the palace. Come dawn, says Xenophon, when hungover Babylonian troops of the garrison in the citadel learned that the Persian army was in the city and Belshazzar was dead, they surrendered—probably talked into it by Gubara, whom Cyrus would soon reward with the post of satrap of Babylonia.

As Babylon awoke to the news that it had been taken by the Persians, virtually without resistance, heralds went throughout the city calling on the population to throw out their weapons. They warned that if any weapons were subsequently found, every occupant of houses concerned would be summarily executed. The vast cache of weapons that was collected was stored away in the citadel. A guard was also placed on the Esagila, in central east Babylon, to keep Persian troops out and protect the religious compound from looting. And the magi of Marduk were permitted to resume daily worship of Marduk at the temple complex.

Meanwhile, Cyrus had remained at his camp north of the city. For one thing, King Nabonidus still remained at large. But once Cyrus learned that Nabonidus was at Borsippa, he marched on that city with part of his army. Berossus says that Nabonidus came into Cyrus's custody before a siege of Borsippa could be commenced. The Cyrus Cylinder says that he was handed over to Cyrus—by the Borsippans, we can suppose.

To demonstrate his respect for the Babylonian royal family, Cyrus ordered full funeral rites performed for Belshazzar, the slain crown prince, sending his own eldest son and crown prince Cambyses to preside over the funeral. He also ordered six days of official mourning for Belshazzar throughout the kingdom and had the bodies of those Babylonians who'd been killed during the night's insurgency given over to their families for burial. Cyrus again showed his magnanimity by sparing Nabonidus, officially crediting Marduk for this. "Marduk, the great lord, bestowed on me as my destiny the great magnanimity of one who loves Babylon."[66]

Berossus says that Cyrus exiled Nabonidus to Carmania, a territory southeast of Babylon and due east of Persis, as vassal king of the region. Nabonidus would owe his loyalty and obedience to Cyrus but would have a small measure of autonomy. Carmania was, and is, a remote and desolate place, a mixture of desert and mountain, albeit a place with a pleasant climate in the elevated portions. Nabonidus had lived happily in semi-retirement in the desert at Tema, so semi-retirement with minimal responsibilities in the wastelands of Carmania may have suited him just as well. There, says Berossus, Nabonidus lived out the rest of his days.

Still Cyrus refrained from entering Babylon. There was the six-day mourning period for Belshazzar to respect, and the march to Borsippa had eaten up several days. But Cyrus wanted to enter his greatest conquest hailed not as a conqueror but as a savior of the people of Babylon, and time was needed for the preparations. It was only on October 26, two weeks after his troops had captured Babylon, that he entered the city to a tumultuous welcome. In one section of the 538 BC Cyrus Cylinder, believed to have been written by priests of Marduk, it is declared: "All the people of Babylon, of all Sumer and Akkad [the Babylonian heartland], nobles and governors, bowed down to him and kissed his feet, rejoicing over his kingship, and their faces shone....They blessed him sweetly and praised his name."

Cyrus had been surprised how downtrodden and poorly fed the people of Babylonia looked as he passed through on his way to Babylon. "The population of the land of Akkad and Sumer, who had become like corpses," he was to say. He blamed this on the rule of Nabonidus, who "brought ruin on them all by a yoke without relief." And he painted himself as the liberator of the Babylonian people. "I soothed their weariness, I freed them from their bonds."[67]

To show that under his new regime life was going to be much better for Babylonians, his arrival in Babylon was marked by a massive feast for all, with "big cattle slaughtered by ax, and many sheep," says the Verse Account of Nabonidus, written by priests of Marduk. It all seems to have had the desired effect. "To the inhabitants of Babylon, a joyful heart is now given," says the Verse Account, sounding like an editorial in a government-controlled newspaper in modern times. "They are like prisoners when the prisons are opened. Liberty is restored to those who were surrounded by oppression. All rejoice to look upon him as king!"

Cyrus had no intention of pillaging or destroying Babylon. Instead he made it his own by making it the center of his empire. A year later, he would proclaim: "I went as a harbinger of peace into Babylon. I founded my sovereign residence within the palace amid celebration and rejoicing."[68] In fact according to Xenophon, from this time forward, when Cyrus was not campaigning, he would spend seven months of each year at Babylon, through the winter, where it was warm and sunny. He would then move to Susa in Elam for three months in spring, with two months at cooler Ecbatana in Media during the height of summer. He would only visit Pasargadae, his ceremonial capital in Persis, seven times during his reign, each time showering money on the women there in remembrance of their role in the victory of the Battle of Pasargadae.

He immediately assumed all the traditional titles of the kings of Babylon so that he could be seen as the latest in a long line of Babylonian sovereigns, not a foreign usurper. From then on, he was officially: "King of the world, great king, powerful king, King of Babylon, King of Sumer and Akkad, King of the Four Quarters of the Earth, son of Cambyses, great king, King of Anshan, descendant of Teispes, great king, King of Anshan, the perpetual seed of kingship."[69]

To show his new Babylonian subjects how devoted he was to Babylon and its protecting god Marduk, he quickly issued orders that kept his occupying troops away from the Esagila and its glittering gold statues and ornamentation. According to the Verse Account of Nabonidus, he also had incense provided so that it could once more burn in the previously abandoned Esagila and ordered the increase in the daily offerings to Marduk at the temple complex. He himself would declare that he multiplied the number of geese, ducks, and pigeons of the offerings. He personally paid daily obeisance to the statues of Marduk and other gods. "He constantly prayed to the gods," the priests of Marduk would write, "prostrated on his face."[70]

Cyrus also set a taxation rate on the city that would not be too burdensome on Babylonians. Xenophon says that in addition to paying the cost of a permanent guard, which he stationed in the city's citadel, Cyrus required his new satrapy of Babylon to pay the cost of maintaining his field army for four months of the year. Other satrapies around the empire paid the balance. And Cyrus quickly set about very visible construction works in Babylon, drafting the locals into the work. The Verse Account says, "He conceived the idea of repairing the city, and he himself took up hoe, spade, and water-basket [for brick-making] and began to complete the wall of Babylon. With a willing heart, the inhabitants executed the original plan of Nebuchadnezzar. He [Cyrus] built the fortifications on the Imgur-Enlil Wall."

The Imgur-Enlil Wall was the city's inner defensive wall, and the official receipt for this work was among documents from Cyrus's administration, written on clay tablets, archaeologists have unearthed. This has led some historians to speculate that the wall was damaged in a Persian assault. However, there is no historical account of an attack that damaged or breached the inner wall. And the report specifically says that Cyrus built fortifications on the wall, meaning he strengthened the existing defenses. He himself says he did this as part of his works during the first year of his rule over the Babylonians: "I strove to increase the defenses of the city wall, and completed the quay of baked brick on the bank of the moat, which an earlier king had built but not completed."[71] The quay work would have been done before the levy in the Euphrates north of the city was removed and the river allowed to resume its former flow and depth through the city.

Cyrus went on to describe work he had carried out on the Esagila. The wall of the complex seems to have been in an unfinished or dilapidated state, for Cyrus talks of completing the wall with baked brick and bitumen and of adding cedar doors with bronze cladding and threshold slabs and door fittings with copper parts—apparently after Nabonidus had removed the doors a decade earlier. Cyrus's work on the Esagila seems to have been quite extensive, for his workmen unearthed an old inscription in its foundations. He was to note, "I saw within it an inscription of Ashurbanipal, a king who preceded me."[72] Ashurbanipal was an Assyrian king who'd ruled Babylon, then part of his Neo-Assyrian Empire, during his 668 BC to 627 BC reign.

In the second year after his conquest of Babylon, Cyrus completed his construction and repair work by inserting the Cyrus Cylinder into the foundations of the Esagila as a sort of time capsule. On the cylinder, he describes representatives coming to Babylon from every quarter of the new Persian Empire, "from the Upper Sea [Black Sea] to the Lower Sea [Indian Ocean]," and "all of them brought their weighty tribute." This is likely to have been for a ceremony during which he celebrated the revitalization of the Esagila and of Babylon as a whole.

On the Cyrus Cylinder, too, Cyrus describes how he returned to their original homes those statues of gods Nabonidus had brought to Babylon, gods "whose sanctuaries had been abandoned for a long time." He named the cities and regions involved, all of them being east of the River Tigris: Ashur, Susa, Akkad, Eshnunna, Zamban, Meturna, and Der as far as the province of Gutium. He added, "I gathered their inhabitants and returned them to their dwellings." These were inhabitants Nebuchadnezzar had previously forcibly relocated to Babylon and its surrounds.

The separate Verse Account of Nabonidus corroborates Cyrus's repatriation of the statues. "The images of Babylon's gods, male and female, he returned to their temple chambers. The gods who'd abandoned their chapels he returned to their mansions. Their wrath he appeased, their mind he put to rest. Those whose power was at a low he brought back to life."

What Cyrus didn't say on his Cyrus Cylinder was that he also took active and immediate steps to eradicate all works, memories, and legacies of Nabonidus. In the Verse Account, priests of Marduk, now restored to prominence by Cyrus, joyfully tell us: "Cyrus effaced Nabonidus's deeds, and everything that Nabonidus constructed. All the sanctuaries of his royal rule, Cyrus has eradicated. The ashes of the burned buildings, the wind carried away." This means that Cyrus burned to the ground the Sin-related temples that Nabonidus had rebuilt in Harran, Sippar, and elsewhere. That wasn't all. "Nabonidus's picture he effaced. In all the sanctuaries, the inscriptions of that name are erased. Whatever Nabonidus had created, Cyrus fed to the flames."

This was all clever propagandizing. It showed Cyrus as a king to be loved, not feared, who was wiping away all signs of the previous oppressive regime. And he backed his words with deeds. This propaganda worked like a charm. The Babylonian people quickly came to revere him. There would be four attempted uprisings by Babylonian freedom fighters during the half century that followed his reign, but during Cyrus's lifetime, there was not a single Babylonian revolt.

18

CYRUS FREES THE JEWS OF BABYLON

THE BOOK OF DANIEL says that Daniel the Jew once more came to prominence under the new administrator of Babylon. That administrator, we know, was for a short time Gubara, the Assyrian provincial governor who had defected to Cyrus and subsequently led the commando raid that resulted in the capture of Babylon. Cyrus rewarded him with the post of satrap of Babylonia, but he was not to live much longer, apparently dying in office, as soon as the first year after the Persian conquest of Babylon.

In Daniel, it says the man in charge of Babylon at this point was Darius the Mede, and it also describes him as "King" Darius. No Mede was king of Babylon, and the first King Darius to rule over Babylon would be Darius I, aka Darius the Great, a Persian. At this point, the future King Darius was just eleven years old, and his reign would not commence for another seventeen years, starting when he was twenty-eight. Yet, Daniel says, incorrectly, that he succeeded Belshazzar. Daniel further muddies the historical waters by saying that this Darius was the son of Ahasuerus. Darius the Great's father was, of course, Hystaspes, and Ahasuerus, who is mentioned several times in the Old Testament, is generally believed by scholars to refer to Xerxes, Darius's *son*.

A number of scholars believe that the figure referred to in Daniel 5 and 6 was, in fact, confused by its author/s with Gubara the governor. It is also possible that the biblical text was referring to another member of the Persian royal family. A clay tablet dating back to the first year after Cyrus's conquest of Babylon refers to his son Cambyses as king of Babylon. This could be taken to mean that, for a time after the death of Gubara, the role of satrap of Babylonia was filled by Cambyses, despite his youth. With Cyrus living at Babylon for seven months of the year, he would have been able to keep a close eye on the satrap.

The book of Daniel later says that Daniel prospered in the reigns of both Cyrus and Darius, which enables the events described in Daniel 6 to be placed in Cyrus's reign, especially as they take place immediately following the death of Belshazzar. All things considered, the historical probability is that the "Darius the Mede" in Daniel was either Gubara the governor, who we know to have been in charge of Babylonia immediately following the death of Belshazzar, or his unidentified successor, who may have been Cambyses. As it's impossible to determine with any certainty this figure's identity, he will be referred to here simply as "the governor."

The story told in the book of Daniel is that not long after Babylon fell to the Persians, Daniel presented himself to the new Persian governor and told him about his past service to Nebuchadnezzar and his short-lived appointment by Belshazzar. According to Daniel, the governor appointed one hundred and twenty officials to administer the satrapy, and over them he placed three deputy governors who reported directly to him. Impressed by Daniel, he offered him the job of the most senior of this trio of deputy governors, and Daniel accepted.

The two other deputy governors and other government officials, many of whom had probably also served the Babylonian
monarchy, were jealous of their boss, this Jew who was put over
them. Unable to find fault with Daniel's work or loyalty, several
went to the governor and convinced him to sign a decree making
it unlawful for any man to make a petition to any god or any man
other than the king for thirty days, with any guilty party to be cast
into a den of lions. Without realizing this was aimed at Daniel, the
perhaps young and naive governor—if it was indeed Cambyses—
signed the decree.

Before long, Daniel's enemies caught him in the act of praying
to Yahweh, asking for God's help, and informed the governor that
he was doing this three times a day, in contravention of the decree.
The governor found himself in a quandary. He liked Daniel. But
Daniel had broken the law he'd been tricked into enacting. The
governor, finding he had no choice, one evening had Daniel placed
in a den where lions were kept, telling him to pray for salvation as
the round door was rolled into place. The governor went back to
the palace. Unable to eat or to listen to the customary music that
was provided at dinner time, he spent a sleepless night worrying
that his favorite would be harmed.

Come dawn, the governor was back at the den. When the stone
door was rolled away, Daniel emerged, unharmed. And the governor was "exceedingly glad." Daniel was to claim that God had sent
an angel who closed up the lions' mouths. Of course, all the governor
had to do to save his deputy was ensure that the lions had been very
well fed before Daniel was put among them. Glutted lions would
show no interest in Daniel if he lay in a corner and kept silent and
still. According to the book of Daniel, the governor then summoned
Daniel's accusers and cast them into the den, along with their wives
and children, and the lions "broke all their bones in pieces." No one
would be informing on Daniel after that!

The book of Daniel says that the governor then had a decree

sent throughout the kingdom in which he proclaimed "the God of Daniel" to be "the living God," a god who had saved Daniel from the lions. For this to have genuinely happened, the governor must have converted to Judaism and then broadcast it to the world—a very dangerous course. Or Daniel had given him the impression that he'd prayed to Marduk, the "living god" referred to in the decree—a very sneaky course. Neither is likely. Most scholars believe this famous Bible story to have been a fabrication. Nonetheless, Daniel was now cemented into his senior post in the administration. "So this Daniel prospered in the reign of Darius, and in the reign of Cyrus," it says in Daniel.

Elsewhere in the Old Testament, the book of Ezra tells us that while Daniel lived on in Babylon, other Jews were returning to Jerusalem. Ezra is believed to have been written by a Babylonian-born Jewish scribe who lived at Babylon until the seventh year of the reign of Persian king Artaxerxes I—458 BC. At that point, Artaxerxes gave him permission to relocate to Jerusalem. According to Ezra, Cyrus had originally given Jews living in Babylonia permission to return to Jerusalem in the first year of his reign over Babylon.

Ezra says that Cyrus issued a written proclamation in which he said, "The Lord God of heaven has given me all the kingdoms of the earth, and he has charged me to build him a house at Jerusalem, which is in Judah." He went on to decree that Jews wishing to return to Jerusalem to rebuild the Temple not only had his permission to do so but were to be supported in the act by his royal treasury.

Romano-Jewish author Josephus, writing in the first century, included in his Jewish Antiquities what he purported to be the text of the letter from Cyrus to Sisennes, his satrap of western Syria and Phoenicia. Josephus says that Cyrus gave specific instructions to Sisennes and Zerubbabel (also written Zorobabel and Zorobel), the Jew Cyrus had appointed to govern the sub-province of

Yehud Medinata, as the kingdom of Judah had been called since the time of the Assyrians. Sisennes was to help the returning Jews with financial and material aid to build their Temple and physically supervise the construction of a structure sixty cubits high and sixty cubits across.

This letter from Cyrus is first mentioned in Ezra, and Josephus clearly used that as the basis for what he purports to be the verbatim text. Josephus often invented the texts of letters and speeches in his writings, which covered thousands of years of Jewish history, with his telltale catchphrase, "the habitable world," often put in the mouths of his historical figures. He also wasn't averse to varying from his source material to paint a picture that agreed with his attitudes. For example, when retelling the book of Genesis in his Jewish Antiquities, he couldn't bring himself to acknowledge that God had spoken directly to a woman as described in Genesis, so he changed the text and had God talking exclusively to men.

Furthermore, Ezra tells us that Sisennes, also known as Tattenai, was satrap of Phoenicia and western Syria during the reign of Darius, two decades after the first year of Cyrus's reign. Clay tablet records prove that in 502 BC, the twentieth year of Darius's reign, Tattenai (called Tattanu in Persian) was indeed governor of this satrapy, which was known as Eber-Nari, literally meaning Across-the-River—the river in question being the Euphrates. It's simply not credible that a satrap would have held his satrapy for fifty-six years through the reigns of four Persian kings or that Tattenai/Sisennes had been governor in 558 BC.

Ezra further knocks on the head the idea that Cyrus ordered Tattenai/Sisennes to facilitate the rebuilding of the Temple by telling us that during the second year of the reign of Darius, Tattenai turned up at Jerusalem to find the work on the Second Temple almost complete and demanded to know what was going on and who had given permission for the work. More on this later, during the reign of Darius.

The point here is that no historical evidence exists for Cyrus giving written permission for the Jews to rebuild their Temple. However, most scholars agree that by September or October 538 BC, the time of the annual Feast of the Tabernacles, a number of Jews had returned from Babylon to Jerusalem with Cyrus's permission. Ezra says that the elders of the tribes of Judah and Benjamin and the priests of the tribe of Levi, led by the high priest Joshua, headed the return and that Cyrus appointed a descendant of the royal house of Judah, Zerubbabel, to govern Judah.

Confusingly, Ezra briefly mentions that another descendant of the royal house of Judah named Sheshbazzar also received the same commission from Cyrus. Scholarly opinions about Sheshbazzar range from suggestions that he was in fact Zerubbabel's uncle Shenazzar, who is mentioned in the biblical book of Kings, that he filled the post of Jewish governor of Yehud Medinata before or after Zerubbabel, that he assisted and supported Zerubbabel, and that Sheshbazzar was another name for Zerubbabel. Certainly, Sheshbazzar soon disappears from the Old Testament, and it is Zerubbabel who governs Yehud Medinata in the continuing narrative.

Zerubbabel, whose name was Babylonian and apparently meant "the seed of Babylon," was the grandson of Jeconiah, second-last in the line of Jewish kings of Judah prior to Nebuchadnezzar's destruction of Jerusalem. Ezra also says that Cyrus instructed Mithradata, his otherwise unknown ganzabara, or treasurer, to return to the Jews the temple artifacts looted by Nebuchadnezzar and place them in Sheshbazzar/Zerubbabel's care until they could be safely deposited at Jerusalem.

Ezra puts the number of Jews who returned from Babylonia at 42,360, plus 7,337 male and female slaves and thousands of horses, mules, camels, and asses carrying their baggage. Scholars dispute that number, with some believing that perhaps 30,000 returned. And historians agree the repatriation was not en masse but was spread over a number of years. It's believed that the bulk of the Jews returned in dribs and drabs between 538 and 520 BC.

A number of Jews who had made comfortable lives for themselves remained in Babylonia, and there would still be a large and vibrant Jewish community in the Babylon region by the first century AD, when it was part of the Parthian Empire, and when Romano-Jewish author Josephus was writing about these events. It was clearly only the most homesick, the most religious, and the most nationalistic Jews who made the return in the reign of Cyrus, including a number who had been born in Babylonia.

Ezra the scribe, a Babylonian-born Jewish priest, would only relocate to Jerusalem a century later, leading a party of priests, their assistants, members of the tribe of Levi, singers, and porters on a trek that took them close to four months. The book of Ezra tells of receiving a written authorization from Persia's King Artaxerxes to travel and to carry silver and gold to Jerusalem and to settle there. Similarly, the very first Jewish returnees must have made the journey with the written permission of Cyrus. Parties of hundreds or thousands of Jewish refugees, driving their animals with them, would have attracted the attention of the Persian authorities along the way, seemingly making a letter of authority mandatory. However, no such letter would be retained by the returnees at Jerusalem.

Did Cyrus allow Jews to return to Jerusalem because the God of the Jews moved him to do so, as the Old Testament would have us believe? No scholar or historian believes this to be the case. As far as we know, to Cyrus, the "Lord God of heaven" mentioned in Ezra was Bel, the Babylonians' Marduk, the Persians' Mithra. To explain Cyrus's sympathy for the Jews, some scholars have speculated that Cyrus may have worshipped the god of Zarathustra, the Mesopotamian priest whose monistic faith lives on today as Zoroastrianism. This faith worships a single god, known as Ahuramazda to the Persians. These scholars suggest that Cyrus equated the Jews' Yahweh with Ahuramazda. However, there is no proof of this.

We know from inscriptions that, decades later, Darius I worshipped Ahuramazda, as did his grandfather Arsames and great-grandfather Ariaramnes before him. Yet Cyrus is only on record worshipping Marduk. French scholar Francois Vallat is convinced that Cyrus was taught to follow Mithra while growing up in Media and equated him with Marduk; Cyrus's foster father, Mithradates, was named after Mithra, and Astyages and his court worshipped Mithra.[73] On the Cyrus Cylinder, which we know to be genuine and contemporary, Cyrus states unambiguously that he believed that Marduk chose him to liberate Babylon and restore the worship of Marduk:

> He [Marduk] inspected and checked all the countries seeking for the upright hand of Cyrus, King of the city of Anshan, and called him by name, proclaiming him aloud for the kingship over everything. He made the land of Guti and all the Median troops prostrate themselves at his feet while he shepherded in justice and righteousness for the black-headed people whom he had put under his care. Marduk, the Great Lord, who nurtures his people, saw with pleasure his fine deeds and true heart.

The content of the Cyrus Cylinder is clearly religious and political propaganda aimed at the inhabitants of Babylonia. But the references on the Cylinder, and in the Verse Account of Nabonidus, to Cyrus restoring and increasing Marduk's observances and to personally prostrating himself daily before the statues of the Babylonian gods indicate either a genuine faith or a cynical exploitation of a faith in which he did not believe. There is no evidence to support the latter view. Indeed, everything points to Cyrus being a devoted worshipper of Marduk/Mithra.

The book of Isaiah states that the God of the Jews said: "Cyrus, he is my shepherd, and shall perform all my pleasure; even saying to Jerusalem, you shall be rebuilt, and to the temple, your foundation will be laid. So said the Lord to his anointed, to Cyrus, whose right hand I have held, to subdue nations before him." This reference in Isaiah is the only time in the Bible that any non-Jew is described as "anointed" by God, and it sets Cyrus apart as a good man chosen by Yahweh to help the Jewish people. Yet, no scholar believes that Cyrus converted to Judaism.

It's interesting to compare the above passage from Isaiah about God choosing Cyrus to be his instrument to the passage on the earlier Cyrus Cylinder, where Marduk is described as choosing Cyrus to be his instrument. The general tenor and turns of phrase are very similar in both Isaiah and the Cyrus Cylinder: "seeking for the upright hand of Cyrus"/"Cyrus, whose right hand I have held," for example. And several words such as "pleasure" and "shepherd/shepherding" appear in both. Christians are very familiar with the term "shepherd" as a consequence of the popular nineteenth-century hymn "The Lord is my Shepherd," which is based on Psalm 23, but as Professor David Richter points out in the Afterword of this book, the term "shepherding" is sparingly used in the Old Testament.

It's not impossible that the author of Isaiah saw the proclamation from the Cyrus Cylinder and borrowed from it. We know that the Cyrus Cylinder proclamation was copied onto flat clay tablets and distributed outside Babylon, as two fragments from such copies have been found at the site of the Babylonian town of Dilbat, modern Dulaim, twenty miles due south of Babylon. The British Museum's chief scholar on the subject of the cuneiform texts of Mesopotamia, Irving Finkel, firmly believes that Cyrus Cylinder text copies like these were distributed throughout Babylonia, and possibly throughout the entire Persian Empire. These copies would have been read aloud and displayed in public places to transmit the words and will of the king to his subjects. A copy would also have been sent to the official archives at Ecbatana, where a Jewish scribe working in the Persian civil service would have had access to it. One way or another, it's not impossible that the author of Isaiah was influenced by the Cyrus Cylinder text.[74]

Cyrus's return of the Jews to their homeland, although not mentioned in any other source apart from Jewish texts, is believed by scholars to have been factual and in accord with the return of the displaced persons from east of the Tigris. The Jews of Babylon, once they heard of the other repatriations, would have put their case to Cyrus, who Xenophon says spent much time in Babylon receiving delegations from the ordinary people of Babylonia and listening to their requests and grievances.

Why would Cyrus permit the Jews to return to Jerusalem? It should be remembered that the sub-province of Yehud Medinata was only small and inconsequential, extending for no farther than some twenty miles around Jerusalem. Herodotus tells us that Cyrus had in mind invading Egypt. That being the case, it would be advantageous to have a way station at Jerusalem and have the crops of Yehud planted and harvested, to help provide sustenance for his army before it crossed the Negev en route to Egypt. Cyrus was a pragmatic ruler and above all, a soldier.

To have returned to Jerusalem by September or October in 538 BC, the first Jewish returnees would have departed Babylon in the spring of that year, once rivers and streams clogged with winter ice and swollen by mountain snow melt had become fordable. And in the spring of 538 BC, Cyrus was distracted. It was then that his first wife and true love, Cassandana, passed away. Distraught, he ordered six days of national mourning for his queen, which according to the Nabonidus Cylinder took place between March 21 and March 26. Cyrus's own mourning would have lasted much longer and perhaps never ended. It's been speculated that he buried Cassandana at Pasargadae.

Cyrus's restoration of the sanctuaries of gods east of the Tigris has convinced some that Cyrus not only allowed the Jews to return to Jerusalem but that he also permitted them to rebuild their Temple at Jerusalem as Ezra and Josephus claim. But there is no firm evidence of this. Why would Cyrus authorize it? The sanctuaries east of the Tigris restored by him were for Marduk and associated deities. The Jerusalem Temple was for an entirely foreign god— unless the Jews were able to convince Cyrus that Yahweh was a manifestation of Marduk in the same way that Marduk was seen as a manifestation of Mithra, and they intimated that they intended to build a temple to Bel.

By 537 BC, Zerubbabel and his fellow returnees had erected an altar precisely where the altar had stood in the Temple of Solomon. Over the following two years, the extensive burned debris of the original temple was removed, and in 535 BC work commenced on the Second Temple, with foundations mapped out and the first stones laid with great rejoicing. In all probability, this gradual work on the Temple's restoration during the reign of Cyrus went forward without the permission or knowledge of Cyrus or his regional satrap, the chief of the satrapy of Eber-Nari.

In Samaria, the old Kingdom of Israel, which roughly equates with today's West Bank, Samaritan descendants of Joseph and Levi learned of the returnees' plan to rebuild the Temple at Jerusalem, and they offered to help. The Samaritans had not rebelled against Nebuchadnezzar and had continued to live in their traditional homeland while the Jerusalemites had lived in exile in Babylonia. In response to their offer of help, Zerubbabel and the Jewish elders turned them down flat. "You have nothing to do with us," these descendants of Judah, Benjamin, and Levi told the Samaritans, whom they accused of being impure through intermarriage with non-Jews, adding that only they, the Jews of Jerusalem, had been expressly instructed by Cyrus to build this temple.

Ezra tells us that the rejected Samaritans began a harassment campaign, frustrating the building activities of the small community of returned exiles at Jerusalem. The Samaritans would build their own temple, on Mount Gerizim, near today's Nablus, where they said Abraham took his son Isaac for sacrifice—the Jerusalem Jews believed that site to be Mount Moriah, which became the Temple Mount. The Samaritans also hired emissaries to make complaints to the administrators of Eber-Nari, eventually going all the way to Ecbatana and Susa. Ezra says the complainants managed to convince Rehum, a royal chancellor, and Shimshai, a senior scribe, to write to the Persian king's senior advisers:

> The Jews which came up from you to us have come into Jerusalem, building the rebellious and bad city, and are setting up the city walls and have joined the foundations. Be it known to the king that, if this is rebuilt, and the walls set up again, then they will not pay toll, tribute, and customs duty, and so you will damage the royal revenue.

The letter's authors also urged the king's advisers to check the Babylonian official records, where they would find that the Jerusalemites had a long history of rebellion and sedition, which was why Nebuchadnezzar destroyed their city. The Persian king referred to in this letter is named by Ezra as Artaxerxes. But he reigned a century later. Not many lines farther on, this episode is firmly set by Ezra during the reign of Cyrus, and this is where scholars believe it belongs. Ezra goes on to say that the king (Cyrus) wrote back that he'd indeed had the records checked, and the Jews had indeed engaged in insurrection, rebellion, and sedition in times past.

According to Ezra, Cyrus then issued a commandment to Rehum and Shimshai: "Now give orders to make these men cease, and that this city not be built, until another order shall be given by me." If Cyrus had indeed originally ordered the Jews to build a Temple at Jerusalem, he appears to have soon forgotten that he'd done so. Once Rehum and Shimshai received this instruction, they moved quickly, going to Jerusalem with Persian troops to forcibly put a halt to all building work as Cyrus had ordered. Ezra goes on: "Then ceased the work of the house of God which is at Jerusalem. It ceased until the second year of the reign of Darius, king of Persia."

The rivalry between Jerusalem Jews and Samaritan Israelites would never cease, with the Jerusalemites eventually gaining supremacy and destroying the Samaritans' Mount Gerizim temple. Jesus Christ would use the New Testament parable of the Good Samaritan to demonstrate that even a "bad" believer in Yahweh could be a good neighbor.

Meanwhile, Daniel, remaining at Babylon, continued to work in the Persian civil service. In 536 BC, according to the book of Daniel, he'd been in mourning for three weeks, probably for a departed parent, and was beside the River Tigris when he saw a vision of God, who told him He was going to fight with "the prince of Persia" and that "the prince of Greece" would come after. As Professor Richter writes in this book's Afterword, this apparent prediction that the Persian kings would be replaced by Greek conqueror Alexander the Great of Macedon is believed to have actually been written several centuries *after* the events it describes.

We know that in 535 BC, the year the Jews were ordered to stop building at Jerusalem, Cyrus reorganized his satrapies. Yehud Medinata was absorbed into the expanded satrapy of Babylonia and Eber-Nari, which took in southern Mesopotamia and the Levant. From this point on, the satrap of Babylonia and Eber-Nari resided in Babylon, with numerous sub-governors reporting to him. Cyrus, after consolidating his new empire, looked to expand it and eliminate regional threats with new military campaigns.

19

"DO NOT GRUDGE ME MY MONUMENT"

CYRUS CONTINUED HIS WISE and unchallenged rule until 530 BC. Herodotus says there were many stories about how Cyrus died. Xenophon claims he died in bed. Ctesias says he died from battle wounds. Herodotus believed that the following was the most credible account of the death of Cyrus.

In the late fall of 530 BC, Cyrus led his troops into battle against a wild Scythian desert tribe, the Massagetae, which occupied parts of the northeastern frontier of his empire in today's Kazakhstan and Uzbekistan. The Massagetae were led by a queen, Tomyris, who had succeeded her husband on his death. By November, the Massagetae were threatening Persia's northeastern frontier with a massive army of infantry and cavalry.

Cyrus, despite the fact he was now seventy years of age, personally led a large Persian force north to confront the challenge, accompanied by his son Cambyses, Croesus the former king of Lydia, and Hystaspes, father of Darius. Coming to the Araxes River, today the Aras and the border between Iran and Azerbaijan, Cyrus encamped, began work on a floating bridge, and sent Tomyris a message, seeking to marry her.

Seeing this as a ploy, Tomyris invited Cyrus to do battle. She gave him two options: she would march away from the river for three days, allowing the Persians to cross, or Cyrus should march away for three days, allowing her army to cross. After this they would battle. Perhaps she thought that, with winter fast approaching, Cyrus would back off. But once before, against the Lydians, Cyrus had seized the initiative by attacking in winter. He wouldn't be backing down. He called together his advisory council.

All of Cyrus's advisers but one recommended that Cyrus withdraw and allow the Massagetae to cross the river, then wipe them out with their backs to the water. The odd man out was King Croesus, who advised Cyrus to cross the river and do battle in enemy territory, which would allow the Persians to sweep on once they had dealt with the enemy army. Cyrus chose to take Croesus's advice. Retreating when he had such a powerful army was not on his agenda.

Persian law required the king to appoint a successor before embarking on military campaigns, so as his engineers bridged the Araxes, Cyrus named his son Cambyses his successor as king in the event of his death and ordered him to return to Persis, taking Croesus with him as his chief adviser. According to Ctesias, Cyrus also appointed his younger son Bardiya satrap of the Bactrians, Choramnians, Parthians, and Carmanians; he also made his stepson Spitaces satrap of the Derbices and stepson Megabernes satrap of the Barcanians, ordering the latter two to follow the commands of their mother, Cyrus's surviving wife, Amytis, in all things.

Herodotus says that the night after the Persian army made the crossing and established itself on the eastern bank of the Araxes, Cyrus had a dream. In this dream, Darius, Hystaspes's now twenty-year-old son, had wings on his shoulders that encompassed all of Asia and Europe, which unnerved the Persian king. This is the first and only time during Cyrus's life that we hear of him being either superstitious or influenced by dreams. Believing this a premonition that Darius was plotting to overthrow him, Cyrus sent Hystaspes back to Persia to keep an eye on his son there, with orders to present him to Cyrus for questioning once the king had wrapped up the Massagetae campaign.

Cyrus then advanced with his army, marching for a day before implementing a stratagem previously suggested to him by the now departed Croesus. Making camp, he laid out a feast, with copious quantities of wine. Then leaving a weak force to guard the camp, he withdrew with the bulk of the army. A Massagetae force comprising a third of their army led by Tomyris's son Spargapises massacred the guard and overran the camp, and as Cyrus expected, glutted themselves on food and wine. Cyrus then attacked the camp with his entire army. Overwhelming the Massagetae, he took Tomyris's son prisoner. After Cyrus freed Spargapises from his chains, the Massagetae prince succeeded in killing himself. When Tomyris heard of this, she vowed to bathe Cyrus's head in blood.

On December 4, Tomyris led her people into battle. To begin with, both armies loosed arrows at each other. With their quivers empty, both sides charged. Eventually, the Massagetae, who wore armor of brass and gold, gained the upper hand. In close-quarters fighting, their brass battle-axes gave them the advantage. As the majority of the Persian army was cut down and even his Immortals died all around him, Cyrus was killed.

Ctesias says that Cyrus was first of all wounded, only to die two days later from his wounds. This is not impossible; the fighting may have stretched over several days, although Herodotus, our primary source on the battle, indicates it was decided in a single day and that Cyrus's body was found among the mounds of dead following a search initiated on Tomyris's orders. After filling an animal skin with blood, the victorious queen bathed Cyrus's severed head in it, completing her vow.

Herodotus says Cyrus had come to think of himself as immortal, yet despite having never previously lost a battle and despite all his titles, including Great King, Mighty King, and King of the World, he had proven as mortal as the next man. It's believed that Cyrus's body ended up in the Mausoleum of Cyrus at Pasargadae, a simple limestone edifice that still stands today. Originally, it was set in lush gardens and watched over by specially chosen magi.

Cambyses, Cyrus's son and successor, apparently ransomed his father's remains from Tomyris as a part of a peace deal that made the Araxes the border between them. Ctesias reports that Cambyses sent his father's chief eunuch Bagapates to collect the king's body and escort it to Pasargadae for interment there. Arrian tells us that Cambyses personally appointed the first magi who tended and protected his father's mausoleum, and, for hundreds of years, the post was passed from fathers to sons. The magi of the mausoleum received a sheep a day and an allowance for other food and wine, plus a horse a month to be sacrificed to the memory of Cyrus.

Two centuries later, Alexander the Great visited the Mausoleum of Cyrus at Pasargadae after he had taken the city during his conquest of the Persian Empire. Alexander was an admirer of Cyrus—he had read Xenophon's *Cyropaedia*—even though he himself conquered the empire Cyrus had created. On two occasions, Alexander paid homage to Cyrus's tomb. Perhaps superstitious about invading the abode of the dead, he didn't venture inside himself. One of his generals, Aristobulus, was sent in to find out what lay inside.

Aristobulus reported back that he found a golden coffin on a table. But Cyrus's remains had been unceremoniously dumped on the floor by looters. The coffin's golden lid had been stolen, and gold had been chipped from the coffin itself. There was also a golden divan covered with colorful material and with a Babylonian rug draped over it. On the divan, too, were Cyrus's clothes: a Median jacket and trousers, robes dyed in amethyst, purple, and many other colors, as well as scimitars, necklaces, and inlaid ear-rings of gold and precious stones.

Alexander was so furious with the magi for allowing Cyrus's tomb to be desecrated that he had them tortured to determine the looters' identities. When the priests provided no names, he set them free. He also gave Aristobulus the task of returning Cyrus's remains to his sarcophagus, repairing the coffin, and restoring the mausoleum to exactly the way it had been prior to the looting. Once this was done, Alexander had the small doorway sealed with stone, which was then plastered and sealed with the royal seal.

There was an inscription on Cyrus's tomb:

O, man, I am Cyrus, son of Cambyses
who founded the empire of Persia
and ruled over Asia.
Do not grudge me my monument.[75]

20

THE SONS OF CYRUS

WHEN CYRUS'S SON CAMBYSES came to the throne in December 530 BC on the death of his father, he was twenty-nine years of age. Known to history as Cambyses II, he would rule for close to eight years. A heavy drinker, he would take several wives, including two of his own sisters, Atossa and Roxane, whom he wed after his father's death. According to Herodotus, Cambyses had shown signs of mental instability growing up, but once he became king, he made crazy and irrational decisions and "by a great range of proofs" was "raving mad."

Cambyses's symptoms suggest that he was in fact suffering from brain cancer, in the form of a frontal lobe tumor. Symptoms of a frontal lobe tumor include seizures, which Cambyses had suffered since childhood. Other frontal lobe tumor symptoms include a weakness on one side of the body, stumbling, dizziness, and difficulty walking—which Cyrus and his physicians would have associated with epilepsy when he was young and with his drunkenness when he was older. That drunkenness may have been Cambyses's way of self-medicating, to drown the headaches associated with a brain tumor. Other symptoms of a frontal lobe tumor include behavioral and emotional changes and impaired judgment, all of which Cambyses displayed before and after he was king.[76]

Notably, a person suffering from a frontal lobe tumor experiences vision problems, including double vision and abnormal eye movements that are obvious to those around them. This would explain Cyrus's acquisition of the Egyptian eye doctor. But of course, neither he nor his advisers would have linked this eye affliction to Cambyses's seizures. In those times, doctors had little knowledge of brain cancers. The Egyptians were famous throughout the classical world for their ointments, both medicinal and cosmetic, and perhaps the eye doctor's treatment for Cambyses involved just such an eye ointment.

With the symptoms of brain cancer typically waxing and waning, it was probably thought that the Egyptian doctor's treatments were having a beneficial but not lasting effect. As the symptoms never entirely went away and always intensified anew, the doctor's services were permanently required, explaining why he was never allowed to go home to Egypt and remained on Cambyses's staff once he became king.

Cambyses moved his residential capital from Babylon to Susa in Elam, closer to his homeland of Persis, but he maintained the empire's administration at Ecbatana and the ceremonial capital at Pasargadae, where a second royal palace found there is believed to have been built by Cambyses for his occasional visits. According to Ctesias, Cambyses retained his father's senior eunuchs Izabates, Aspadates, and Bagapates as his chief administrators, so that it was business as usual around the empire from the moment Cyrus died.

Apparently unknowing of, or uncaring of, his father's prophetic dream about Darius, son of Hystaspes, Cambyses appointed twenty-year-old Darius to the prestigious court post of *arstibara*, Lance Bearer of the King. Cambyses employed a mature Persian noble by the name of Prexaspes as King's Messenger, and to the important role of Cup Bearer—the same post that Cyrus had held in the court of Astyages—he appointed Prexaspes's son. As for Cambyses's step-brothers Spitaces and Megabernes, we never hear of them again. They may well have continued to govern various satrapies for years to come. Being Medes and not Persian descendants of Achaemenes, they had no claim on the Persian throne. According to Ctesias, their mother Amytis would take her own life by drinking poison during Cambyses's reign.

Under the influence of his father's advisers at the commencement of his reign, Cambyses began by making sensible decisions. Probably on the advice of Croesus, the former king of Lydia his father had appointed Cambyses's chief counselor and who was now aged in his late sixties, Cambyses seems to have secured a peace treaty with Queen Tomyris and her Massagetae, which left his eastern border secure. This allowed him to turn his eyes west, to the conquest of the Greek island states of the Aegean.

The Persians were not sailors, and Persia did not possess a navy. But under Cambyses, the Persian Empire became a major naval power. What Cambyses did was use the fleet of the maritime state of Phoenicia, part of his father's empire, and through alliances add the fleets of the islands of Cyprus and Samos to his navy. This navy proceeded to conquer one Ionian island after another, until by 525 BC, the Persian Empire controlled the Aegean Sea, and the conquered island states sailed for Persia. This enabled Cambyses to launch a campaign in 525 BC that his father had long contemplated: the invasion of Egypt.

The campaign was initiated by, of all people, Cambyses's Egyptian eye doctor. That doctor had long harbored a grudge against Pharaoh Amasis II for separating him from his Egyptian wife and children when he was dispatched to Cyrus's court years before. While Cambyses was still preoccupied with his Aegean conquests, the doctor suggested he request the hand of the pharaoh's daughter in marriage. As far as the doctor was concerned, he was in a win-win situation: if Amasis complied, it would be a great annoyance to him; while, if he didn't, it would be a great annoyance to the easily riled Cambyses, who might take out his anger on Egypt.

Pharaoh Amasis, previously a general in the service of Pharaoh Apries, had led a rebellion against Apries. The deposed pharaoh had fled to Babylon, where his ally King Nebuchadnezzar had given him an army to retake his throne. Apries and his Babylonian army had been defeated in 567 BC by Amasis when they attempted to invade Egypt, and Amasis had killed Apries. To give legitimacy to his rule, Amasis had married one of Apries's daughters. Now, the wily Amasis agreed to Cambyses's wedding proposal, but instead of sending his own daughter to Persia to marry the young king, he sent Nitetis, another daughter of Apries, pretending that she was his own flesh and blood.

Tall and beautiful, Princess Nitetis was also bold, for when Cambyses referred to her father as Amisis once she had become his wife, she corrected him and revealed the truth. Cambyses was understandably furious that the pharaoh had attempted to trick him, and he was considering how to enact his revenge when an Egyptian defector arrived at his court.

That defector was Thanes, a native of Halicarnassus and commander of Greek mercenaries in the Egyptian army. After falling out with Pharaoh Amasis, Thanes had fled from Egypt by ship. Thanes outsmarted an Egyptian eunuch sent to take him captive and presented himself to Cambyses following the Nitetis revelation and shared all the pharaoh's military secrets. He also suggested how a Persian army marching on Egypt could overcome the barrier of the Negev Desert, which would ordinarily involve a waterless march of three days.

All the territory south of the coastal city of Gaza, the home of the Palestinian Syrians, says Herodotus, who visited there while sailing to Egypt, was controlled by the king of Arabia. Send an envoy to the Arabian king, Thanes urged Cambyses; arrange a treaty of friendship, and ask the Arabs to provide water to the Persian army when it reached the desert. This Cambyses duly did. Herodotus says he was told two stories about how the king of Arabia supplied the water for the Persian army's desert crossing. The story he believed had the king loading thousands of camels with filled water-bags made of skins and stationing them across the desert. The other story, which Herodotus didn't find credible, had the Arabs creating a twelve-mile water pipeline made from animal skins that sent water from a lake into the desert.

Once the Arabs provided the solution to the Persians' desert water supply problem, Cambyses sent spies into Egypt. Ctesias says that one of Cambyses's senior eunuchs, Izabates, had a cousin, Combaphis, who was a senior eunuch in the pharaoh's service. Via Izabates, Combaphis secretly agreed to surrender vital bridges to the Persian army when it reached Egypt, in return for appointment as satrap of Egypt once it came under Persian control. In 526 BC, while these arrangements were being made and an invasion force was being prepared, Amasis died after a reign of forty-four years. But Cambyses had set his mind on removing the Egyptian thorn from his side, and the operation went forward.

Amasis's successor was his son Psamtik III, called Psammenitus by Herodotus. He was just six months into his reign when he was alerted that a Persian army was marching on Egypt. Taking the Egyptian army to Pelusium, east of the Nile River, Psamtik made camp and waited for Cambyses to arrive. Cambyses's entourage for the campaign included his younger brother Bardiya.[77] King Croesus was also in the party, as was the Greek mercenary commander Thanes of Halicarnassus, Lance Bearer Darius, King's Messenger Prexaspes and his son the king's Cup Bearer, and the king's sister/wife Roxane, who was by this time pregnant to Cambyses.

The Persian army would have included, in addition to the Persians, Medians, and Elamites of the revitalized Immortals, Persian and Median cavalry. Herodotus says that the bulk of Cambyses's infantry was made up of men from the conquered Greek states of Asia Minor. After the vast force arrived and made camp within sight of the waiting Egyptian army, Pharaoh Psamtik's Greek mercenaries then brought out the sons of Thanes, whom he'd left behind in Egypt, and executed them one at a time in view of their father. The mercenaries then drank the blood of the slain youths.

A "stubborn" battle between the two armies ensued, says Herodotus, but the Persians won the day, and Psamtik was captured alive. Ctesias says that 50,000 Egyptian troops died in the battle as well as 7,000 Persians. Several decades later, Herodotus visited the battle site and was shown the sun-bleached bones and skulls of the dead still lying where the troops of both sides had fallen, in two groups, stripped of their weapons, clothing, and accoutrements.

The Egyptian survivors fled up the Nile to their capital, Memphis, where they closed the gates. When Cambyses sent a ship up the river to offer these Egyptian troops surrender terms, the Egyptians massacred all two hundred aboard. Cambyses laid siege to Memphis, which soon fell. The databara, the Achaemenid judges of Persia accompanying the king, adjudged that ten Egyptians of noble birth must die for every one of those massacred on the ship, starting with Psamtik's son.

When Psamtik himself showed great humility after this sentence was passed, Cambyses, urged by Croesus, ordered the son of the pharaoh spared. But the message arrived too late, after the young man had been executed. Cambyses followed his father's policy of clemency to defeated sovereigns and spared Psamtik and kept him close. But when, only months later, it was discovered that Psamtik was attempting to ferment a revolt by Egyptians, Cambyses put him to death. According to Herodotus, Cambyses also had his vengeance on Amasis, the pharaoh who had striven to trick him, by removing his mummified body from its tomb, desecrating it, then burning it.

The rulers of Libya and the Cyrenaican cities of Cyrene and Barca all sent emissaries submitting to Cambyses, who now "took counsel with himself," says Herodotus, and decided to launch three new North African campaigns almost simultaneously. One was a naval assault on Carthage. This failed when the Phoenicians, the backbone of the Persian navy, refused to go against the Carthaginians because of their shared heritage—Carthage's founder Queen Dido and her first settlers had been Phoenicians.

The second campaign was against the Siwa Oasis in Egypt's Western Desert, home to the oracle of Ammon, which apparently held a fascination for Cambyses. This proved more disastrous than the attack on Carthage—a detachment of 50,000 men from the Persian army reportedly disappeared while crossing the desert toward Siwa. According to the Persian version of the story, a massive sandstorm smothered the entire army. Some modern historians consider this a later Persian cover-up of a defeat by Egyptian rebels. Modern archaeologists' attempts to find traces of the lost army in the desert—remnants of weapons and equipment—have come up empty.

Cambyses's third new campaign was to be a military expedition south of the Egyptian Delta into the kingdom of Kush, today's Sudan, which the Greeks and Persians called Ethiopia. Before embarking on this venture into the unknown, Cambyses sent emissaries to Kush with gifts for its ruler and orders to spy out the lay of the land and the kingdom's military preparedness. The sovereign of Kush wasn't fooled, sending back the Persian envoys with a gift for Cambyses—a massive unslung bow—and a message: "When the Persians can easily pull a bow of such strength, then let them come with an army of superior strength."[78]

According to Herodotus, when Cambyses attempted to string the bow, he failed. It's to be remembered that, if he did indeed suffer from a brain tumor, the limbs on one side of his body would have been weakened. His brother Bardiya then asked if he could try stringing the bow, and he succeeded where Cambyses had failed, angering Cambyses so greatly that he sent Bardiya back to Susa.

Leaving his Greek troops at Memphis as a garrison, Cambyses led the rest of his army into Kush without having made sufficient supply preparations. Food ran out when he was only a fifth of the way into the journey, and his men turned to eating grass. When there was no grass, the troops resorted to cannibalism of their comrades. After Cambyses heard of this, he abandoned the operation and retreated to Memphis, having lost "vast numbers of troops," says Herodotus. There at Memphis on the Nile, Cambyses took up residence, sending the maritime component of his armed forces home.

The now morose and increasingly drunk young king learned that in his absence a live bull had mysteriously appeared in the Temple of Apis, an Egyptian god that took the form of a bull. No doubt the bull was smuggled in by Egyptian priests to inspire worship, which it did, with the populace feasting and dancing throughout Egypt. This enraged Cambyses, who saw it as a celebration of his failed Kush campaign. First executing the officers he'd left in charge at Memphis for allowing this, Cambyses had the Egyptian priests bring the bull to him.

When the animal was led in, Cambyses, probably drunk, immediately jumped up, drew his dagger, and stabbed the bull. Witnesses thought that he intended to stab the bull in the belly but missed, for he plunged the dagger into the animal's thigh. But, in stabbing the bull in the thigh, Cambyses appears to have been emulating the legendary act of Mithra, principal god of the Persians. The bull would eventually die from its wound.

"Blockheads!" Cambyses raged at the priests. "Do you think that gods come like this, of flesh and blood?" He ordered the priests punished, and anyone found celebrating Apis was put to death.[79]

Cambyses had only just begun. Going on a rampage through the temples of Memphis, he turned out mummified bodies and burned them, and he scorned and burned the wooden images of Egyptian gods. Later, once he had sobered up, sensible advisers such as Croesus must have convinced him that alienating his new Egyptian subjects by trashing their ancestors, customs, and religion was no way to maintain control of his latest conquest. We know from archaeological finds that while in Egypt Cambyses now took to wearing the dress of pharaohs and had a monument raised to Apis—on which he had himself depicted kneeling before the god.

Croesus continued to give wise counsel, but he knew that he had to be careful what he said to Cambyses and when, for the young king clearly felt he had a lot to live up to as the son of Cyrus. At dinner one day at Memphis with his senior courtiers including Croesus, Cambyses asked them all, "What sort of a man do you think me compared to my father Cyrus?"

Some courtiers replied that he had surpassed Cyrus because he'd added much territory to the Persian Empire. But Croesus disagreed. "In my judgment, son of Cyrus," said he, "you are not equal to your father." A chilled silence must have filled the room. "For," Croesus went on, "you have not left behind a son such as he did." This response delighted Cambyses.[80]

Nonetheless, the king's erratic behavior continued. According to Herodotus, "Cambyses, who even before had not been quite right in the mind, was, as the Egyptians say, smitten with madness." After dreaming that he received a messenger from Sardis, who informed him that his brother Bardiya had assumed the Persian throne, he instructed Prexaspes, the King's Messenger, to go home to Sardis and kill Bardiya. Herodotus heard two different reports of how Bardiya was subsequently murdered. In one, Prexaspes returned and killed the king's brother in a "hunting accident" outside Susa. In the other, Prexaspes drowned him in the Gulf of Aden, south of Susa. Prexaspes personally buried Bardiya's body, and his death was hushed up.

Once Prexaspes returned to Memphis and reported the removal of Bardiya, the King's Messenger became overconfident. Cambyses asked him—obviously feeling guilty over the murder of his brother, and probably well on the way to being drunk—"What sort of man, Prexaspes, do the Persians think I am?"

"Oh, sire," Prexaspes replied, "they praise you greatly in all things but one—they say you are too much given to the love of wine."

"What!" snapped Cambyses. "They say now that I drink too much wine, and so have lost my senses and have gone out of my mind!" After calling for a bow and arrow from the *vacabara*, his Bow Bearer, he took aim at Prexaspes's son, who stood on duty as Cup Bearer in the distant vestibule to the dining room. "If I shoot and hit him in the middle of the heart, it will be plain the Persians have no grounds for what they say," said Cambyses, sighting along the arrow as his aim wavered. "If I miss him, I accept that the Persians are right, and that I am out of my mind." He let fly, and the arrow hit Prexaspes's son in the heart. The youth fell dead to the stone floor. "Now you can see plainly, Prexaspes," said Cambyses with a grin, "that it's not I who is mad, but the Persians who have lost their senses." Then he laughed. "I pray you, tell me, have you seen a mortal man send an arrow with a better aim?"

Prexaspes, in shock and with rising fear for himself, returned, "Oh, my lord, I don't think that Bel himself could shoot so dexterously."

But Croesus, who was also present, berated the king for yielding to his youth and his temper and told him to control himself.

"Do you presume to offer me advice?" Cambyses raged.

"It's by your father's wish that I offer you advice," Croesus retaliated. "He charged me strictly to give you such counsel as I might see to be for your most good."

"I've long been looking for something against you," said Cambyses, reaching for another arrow.[81]

Unlike the young Cup Bearer, Croesus didn't stand obediently to receive an arrow. As Cambyses fumbled with arrow and bow,

Croesus scampered from the room. Court staff hid him until the king slept off his anger, and the next day, Cambyses declared that he was glad that Croesus had survived and welcomed him back to his court. As for the staff who'd hidden Croesus, Cambyses had them executed.

A little later, Cambyses argued with his pregnant sister/wife Roxane. Herodotus says he heard that Roxane was either unhappy that Cambyses had soiled the reputation of the royal house of Cyrus by marrying her, or she began to cry when reminded of their murdered brother Bardiya. For one reason or another, or perhaps both, Cambyses flew into a rage with Roxane and viciously beat her. Suffering a miscarriage, Roxane died a painful death. Cambyses reportedly received the news of her passing without a tear or any sign of remorse.

Cambyses set off to return to Susa and had just reached a city in Syria, which Josephus identifies as Damascus, when news arrived that in February his dead brother Bardiya had assumed the throne in his absence. Herodotus says that Patizeithes—a noble of the Median tribe called the Magi, not a priestly magus as many have assumed—had been left in charge at Susa by Cambyses, and he'd guessed that Bardiya had been murdered. He had a brother, identified as Gaumata by Darius on the Behistun Inscription, who bore a striking resemblance to Bardiya, and Patizeithes came up with the idea of putting Gaumata on the throne posing as Bardiya.

Before Cambyses could expose the imposter, an accident befell him. In rare agreement, Ctesias and Herodotus say that Cambyses accidentally stabbed himself in the thigh. But Ctesias says this occurred in Babylon while whittling a piece of wood "to fill in time," while Herodotus more credibly places the accident in Syria en route back to Susa and says that, as Cambyses sprang onto a horse to hurry to deal with Gaumata, the bottom of his scabbard broke off and the tip of his sword penetrated his thigh. Gangrene set in, and Cambyses died a slow and agonizing death, taking his last breath in July 522 BC—ten days after receiving the leg wound in Ctesias's version, twenty days later according to Herodotus. Izabates the chief eunuch took Cambyses's body to Persis for interment. When Izabates attempted to tell the troops that an imposter, Gaumata, was pretending to be their king Bardiya, Gaumata ordered him dragged from the temple where he took refuge, and executed.

Gaumata the fake Bardiya, secluding himself at a castle in the Median mountains between Ecbatana and Halwan, and locking away Cambyses's sister Atossa to prevent her exposing him, ruled for seven months, decreeing a three-year, empire-wide halt to taxes and military service to gain swift popularity. That September, six Persian Achaemenid nobles led by the courtier Gobryas, who recruited his son-in-law Darius, until recently Cambyses's Lance Bearer, as a seventh member of the conspiracy, went to the castle, burst in on Gaumata while he was in bed with a concubine, and put him to death. Gaumata's brother Patizeithes and other Median nobles supporting the imposter were also executed.

Some historians suggest that the conspirators invented the story of Gaumata the imposter, and the king they killed was the real Bardiya. Others even think the gang of seven previously killed Cambyses and invented the story of his accident. The assassins certainly had good reason to remove Cambyses: self-preservation. The fate of Prexaspes's son and of Roxane and the near death of Croesus were just the tip of the iceberg; before his return from Egypt, Cambyses had buried twelve Persian nobles up to their necks in the sand, on a whim. Nonetheless, Darius's version of events and Herodotus's supporting account stand as the officially recorded story.

Both sons of Cyrus were dead. The seven assassins had agreed that once Gaumata was removed, one of them would take the throne and the other six would loyally serve him. They chose to let Bel decide who the new king would be. The next morning at dawn, the seven would ride toward the rising sun, and the man whose horse neighed first after sunrise would be king. The groom of young Darius found a way to make his horse neigh on cue—perhaps a burr under the saddle—and Darius won the contest and the throne. Cyrus's dream at the Araxes had been realized.

21

DARIUS AND THE
JERUSALEM TEMPLE

A T THE AGE OF TWENTY-EIGHT, Darius I became ruler of the
Persian Empire. He would rule for thirty-six years. During
that time, he would dramatically expand the empire. Boldly building a bridge of boats across the Hellespont, today's Dardanelles, he
would lead a Persian army into southern Europe, bringing Thrace
and Macedonia under Persian rule. He would defeat the Scythians
and push the boundaries of the empire east as far as modern Kara-
chi in Pakistan.

Darius even invaded mainland Greece, striving to punish
Athens for supporting an Ionian revolt in Asia Minor, a revolt
that resulted in the burning of Croesus's former capital, Sardis.
Darius vowed to burn Athens in reprisal for this, but the Persian
invasion of Greece would bring one of Darius's rare defeats: the
famous Battle of Marathon on the coast just northeast of Athens. Darius wasn't in command at Marathon—the Persian army
was led by his Median general Datis. Darius planned to lead the
next attack on Greece, but his failing health intervened. His son

Xerxes would attempt to complete the task. First overwhelming the Spartans at Thermopylae, he saw Athens burn as his father had vowed, only to be defeated by Themistocles and the allied Greek fleet at Salamis.[82]

The Ionian revolt against Darius was no isolated event. Darius's reign was marked by numerous revolts, four in Babylonia alone. The first erupted in Babylon three months after Darius took the throne in September 522 BC, and rebellion soon spread like wildfire throughout the empire, to Asia Minor, Egypt, Media, Elam, and Parthia—where Darius's father, Hystaspes, led its suppression. Revolt even broke out in Darius's native Persis.

Darius's youth may have caused some concern, but the major problem was his perceived legitimacy because he was only distantly related to Cyrus, revered creator of the empire. Persis rebelled because it was intensely loyal to Cyrus's son Bardiya, or the man thought to be Bardiya, and took his assassination badly. Initially Darius did everything he could to assume the mantle of a legitimate successor to Cyrus. He had himself crowned at Pasargadae, the city founded by Cyrus and Cyrus's last resting place. Darius took as his wives two daughters of Cyrus, Atossa and Artystone. Atossa would wield much influence in Darius's court, ensuring that Darius made their son Xerxes his heir, even though he wasn't Darius's firstborn son, so that a descendant of Cyrus took the throne. To establish yet another link with Cyrus, Darius even married Parmida, the young daughter of Bardiya.

Supported by a loyal army and equally loyal lieutenants and basing himself at Ecbatana, Darius systematically put down all the initial revolts by December 521 BC. As stability returned to the empire, Darius was able to extend his control from sea to sea. But in that second year of Darius's reign, the Jews at Jerusalem came into conflict with the Persian administration. With Babylonian rebellion twice severing contact between Eber-Nari and satrapy headquarters in Babylon in 522 and 521 BC, the Jews of Jerusalem recommenced construction of their Temple and city walls. In the opinion of religious scholars Elias Bickerman and Diana Edelman, Zerubbabel and his fellow Jews took advantage of the breakdown in the empire's administration, hoping their rebuilding efforts would escape attention.[83]

But, says the book of Ezra, Tattenai, Persian governor of Eber-Nari, was alerted to the work on the Temple and city walls and turned up at Jerusalem, demanding, "Who has commanded you to build this house, and to make up this wall?"

The Jews refused to stop work, perhaps because they thought the civil unrest throughout the empire might lead to them soon having their freedom. They also refused to give their names, declaring, "In the first year of Cyrus, the king of Babylon, the same king Cyrus made a decree to build this house of god." And they suggested that the king check the records at Babylon for a copy of the decree of Cyrus.[84]

So Tattenai went away and wrote to Darius, telling him all this. The empire's records, going back decades, were all stored at Ecbatana—called Achmetha by the Jewish authors of the Bible. And Darius was then at Ecbatana. According to the book of Ezra: "Then Darius the king made a decree, and search was made in the house of the rolls, where the treasures were laid up in Babylon. And there was found at Achmetha in the palace that was in the province of the Medes, a roll, and in this was a record."

"The house of the rolls" refers to the official archives, and "a roll" refers to a papyrus scroll, but the references to them in relation to Cyrus in Ezra appear to be fundamental errors. Modern experts tell us that while records of this era created in Egypt were written on papyrus—there are surviving Egyptian papyri containing Egypt-related edicts of Cambyses and Darius—all records created at Babylon, Susa, and Ecbatana during the reigns of Cyrus, Cambyses, and Darius were written exclusively on clay tablets. Any decree of Cyrus would have been found on a clay tablet, not on a scroll, or "roll."

There are several potential reasons for this error. Ezra was apparently written during the reign of Persian King Artaxerxes, 465-424 BC, a century after the reign of Cyrus, when papyri records were more widespread, and the author, or authors, of Ezra simply assumed they had been used in the time of Cyrus. Alternatively this chapter was written in Egypt, where Cambyses and Darius had used papyri, with the assumption that Cyrus's Babylonian documents were also written on papyrus. Or, this entire episode was an invention by the Ezra author/s, and there was no such record. Ezra continues:

> In the first year of Cyrus the king, the same Cyrus the king made a decree concerning the house of God at Jerusalem, "Let the house be built, and the place where they offer sacrifices, and let its foundations be strongly laid; the height to be sixty cubits, and the breadth sixty cubits, with three rows of great stones and a row of new timber, and let the expenses be provided by the king's palace."

It went on to say that Cyrus also ordered the Temple treasures looted by Nebuchadnezzar returned to the Jews of Jerusalem.

Based on this decree, Darius ordered Tattenai the governor to permit the Jews to continue building their Temple and to provide expenses for Temple offerings from the taxation revenues of Eber-Nari. In an inscription at his tomb at Mount Behistun—also written Bisotun and Begistun and meaning "Mountain of the Gods"—Darius credits Ahuramazda with helping him overcome the pretender Gaumata, and some scholars have postulated that Darius, a confessed follower of the Persian solo god Ahuramazda, had sympathy for the Jews, who also worshipped a single god. However, a zealous follower of one god would surely deny the existence of all other professed gods. It seems more likely that Darius let the Jews proceed because he was keen during these rebellious times to associate himself with any act of Cyrus. And possibly he'd been led to believe that the Jews would be dedicating their Temple to Ahuramazda, his "Lord of the heavens."

The Jews of Jerusalem joyfully proceeded, completing their Second Temple in 516 BC. In the late first century BC, Herod the Great, king of Judea, the by-then expanded former kingdom of Judah, and a Roman vassal state, would massively rebuild and expand the Temple in what some scholars rate as the world's largest construction project of that era.

In 516 BC, as the basic Second Temple was completed, King Darius was two years into his own massive construction project, his new Persian capital, Persepolis, some fifty miles from Pasargadae. By then in the sixth year of his reign, Darius continued to refer to Cyrus's family as "our family" but had cut loose from Cyrus to establish his own royal credentials; on the Behistun Inscription he stressed that he, too, was a direct descendant of Achaemenes and Teispes, founders of the Achaemenid ruling family.

So, was the edict of Cyrus that Darius endorsed genuine? It does seem odd that, back in 535 BC, three years after Cyrus supposedly permitted the Jews to rebuild their Temple with the above edict, he seemed to have forgotten all about it when he ordered all Jewish construction at Jerusalem to halt. Could the copy of the edict found at Ecbatana have been a forgery? That is possible, especially if it was presented on a papyrus scroll, which we know to have been an anachronism.

There is no way of verifying the authenticity of this copy of the Cyrus decree, but it is interesting to note that according to the book of Esther, King Darius had a very senior Jewish assistant by the name of Mordecai, who resided at Susa. Esther tells of how Mordecai rose to become Darius's right-hand man. According to the Jewish Talmud, Mordecai's full name was Mordecai Bilshan. Marduka was the Persian title of several highly placed officials in Darius's administration, and some scholars suggest that Mordecai's Persian name was Bilshan the Marduka.

According to the Talmud, too, Mordecai was a prophet, who began to prophesy in the second year of Darius's reign, just at the time that the copy of the Cyrus decree was found. Like all the Jews of the Babylonian captivity, Mordecai would have been multilingual. He would have spoken Hebrew, Persian, Elamite, perhaps Akkadian, and certainly Aramaic—the international language of the Jews and the standardized language of Persian official records. Was Mordecai in a position to organize a forged letter to help his fellow Jews at Jerusalem get out of hot water when they were discovered rebuilding the Temple? He certainly was.

This is not to say the forging of the Cyrus decree, if it indeed occurred, was a bad thing. The Jews were captives. Their faith had been suppressed, and they were forced to bow down to foreign gods Bel and Nabu. Foreign invaders occupied their land, and even when Cyrus permitted some Jews to return home, they were subject to the orders, restrictions, and whims of a distant administration. To forge the Cyrus decree to permit the reconstruction of the Temple of Yahweh, at a time when Darius was preoccupied with empire-wide rebellions and their aftermath, would have been both clever and bold.

EPILOGUE

Was Cyrus Great?
And Is There a Modern Parallel?

O N OCTOBER 12, 1971, the Shah, or king, of Iran, Moham-mad Reza Pahlavi, commenced a massive, enormously expensive, and spectacular ceremony at the ruins of Cyrus the Great's capital, Pasargadae and Persepolis. The Shah was celebrating the 2,500th anniversary of the founding of the Persian Empire by Cyrus. As part of this ceremony, several days later members of the Iranian military, dressed and armed as soldiers of Cyrus' army, paraded past the Shah, and the Shah and other dignitaries laid wreaths at the foot of Cyrus's tomb. In doing this, the Shah was attempting to associate his ruling Pahlavi dynasty and Iran as a whole with Cyrus, in part to stem the rise of Islamic nationalism in his country. His efforts, and his money, were wasted. Less than eight years later, the Shah had fled the country and his regime was toppled by the revolution that turned Iran into an Islamic republic.

Cyrus, the Shah's pinup boy, was seemingly erased from Iranian history under the Islamic ayatollas. But then, in 2010, the sixth president of the Islamic Republic of Iran, the eccentric, erratic, and unpredictable Mahmoud Ahmadinejad, opened an exhibition at the National Museum of Iran in Tehran. That exhibition was centered on the Cyrus Cylinder, the original of which was on loan to Iran from the British Museum for four months. In opening the exhibition, President Ahmadinejad extolled Cyrus and declared that the Cyrus Cylinder was history's first charter of human rights, which was ironic, considering the many accusations from human rights watchdogs that Ahmadinejad routinely trampled on the rights of his own citizens.

A replica of the Cyrus Cylinder had been presented to the United Nations by the Pahlavi regime just two days after the Shah's 1971 ceremony at Pasargadae. Called the "Edict of Cyrus," it remains on display at the UN headquarters in New York City to this day, where, echoing President Ahmadinejad, it is described as the first human rights declaration. That claim is somewhat hyperbolic. The Cylinder's content is neither an edict, i.e., a command or law, nor a human rights declaration. It is for the most part a statement by and about Cyrus describing past actions by both him and King Nabonidus, with the assertion that Cyrus was chosen by Bel to overthrow Nabonidus. The balance of the Cylinder's text takes the form of a prayer to multiple gods. As for the reference to freeing captive peoples and the restoration of their temples, this only covers people from east of the Tigris River who worshipped the god Marduk, the same deity whom Cyrus, on the Cylinder, professes to worship. The Cyrus Cylinder is in reality an early example of political propaganda. The Shah and President Ahmadinejad in turn used the Cylinder and Cyrus for their own political propaganda purposes.

We only have to fast forward another six years to the next examples of Cyrus the Great being used as the subject of modern political propaganda. As Professor Richter points out in the following Afterword, during the 2016 US presidential primaries some American evangelical Christian leaders likened Donald Trump to Cyrus. By October 2018, a month before the US midterm elections, a thousand theaters across the country were screening *The Trump Prophecy*, a film produced by the religious right in which, citing God's anointing of Cyrus in Isaiah 45, Donald Trump, forty-fifth president of the United States, is chosen by God to save His people. "Trump as Cyrus is the model for a nonbeliever appointed by God as a vessel for the purposes of the faithful," explained columnist Katherine Stewart in the *New York Times*.[85]

As Professor Richter also reminds us, when President Trump moved the American embassy in Israel from Tel Aviv to Jerusalem in 2018, Israel's prime minister Benjamin Netanyahu referenced Cyrus in praising Trump for making the move. A year later, Netanyahu again referenced Cyrus as one of the "historic giants who helped secure the future of the Israeli people," when the Jewish prime minister once more praised President Trump, this time for recognizing Israel's sovereignty over the Golan Heights.[86]

So are Cyrus and Trump worthy of connection, and of such praise? Can the two men be favorably compared? One Christian pastor voiced the view of many evangelicals when he said in 2018 that, like Cyrus, Mr. Trump was "used as an instrument of God for deliverance," despite the fact that Trump was "this flawed human being like you or I, this imperfect vessel, and He's using him in an incredible, amazing way to fulfil His plans and purposes."[87]

Unlike some other historical figures such as Rome's Pompey the Great, Cyrus was not known by the title Great in his own lifetime. His official title did include "Great King," but this was also the case with his predecessors and successors. The title Cyrus the Great was bestowed upon him much later by Western historians, in part to distinguish him from his grandfather Cyrus I and the later Cyrus III, called Cyrus the Younger by historians, who ineptly and unsuccessfully attempted to wrest the Persian throne from his brother Artaxerxes II in 401 BC.

Nonetheless, Cyrus was by any measure a great man. A bold and brave soldier, he led his men from the front when opponents stood back and let others do the fighting. He sought counsel from subordinates and took their advice. But he was not a consensus man; Cyrus took what he adjudged to be the best idea in the room and ran with it. Some of his cleverest ideas were the suggestions of others—Harpagus's camel trick and Oebares's dummy soldiers among them. Cyrus was a master organizer. The efficient Persian civil service he established served his successors well for hundreds of years. Cyrus was revered and respected throughout his empire, and was admired long after his passing by adversaries of the Persians such as Alexander the Great. Cyrus showed a magnanimity toward conquered enemy leaders that was almost unique in human history. Julius Caesar claimed to be magnanimous, yet he still executed opponents such as Gallic Revolt leader Vercingetorix, even chopping off the hands of every man in a rebel Gallic city. That was not magnanimity at work.

Cyrus put his magnanimity down to the influence of Marduk, god of the Babylonians, equivalent of the Persians' Mithra. His devotion to Marduk is his only recorded religious affiliation. There is no proof that, like Darius, he worshipped Ahuramazda. In fact, authorities such as the Iranian Heritage Foundation are in no doubt that, due to his Median/Persian upringing, Cyrus worshipped Mithra.[88] How then to explain his approval of the return of Jewish exiles to Jerusalem and permission for them to rebuild a temple dedicated to a foreign god?

Some scholars credit that return of the Jewish exiles to a broad policy of Cyrus's of repatriating peoples exiled by Nebuchadnezzar and granting the restoration of their temples. There was no such broad policy. We know only of Cyrus returning peoples who had originated east of the Tigris, people of similar ethnic backgrounds to himself, like the Elamites, and who worshipped Marduk/Mithra. The Jews were from the far west of Cyrus's empire and worshipped an alien deity.

It's to be remembered that the Jews and the ruined city of Jerusalem comprised only a very small, insignificant part of Cyrus's empire. They were considered so unimportant that none of the Greek writers such as Herodotus, Xenophon, or Ctesias ever mentioned them—even though Herodotus is known to have visited Palestine and parts of the Persian Empire such as Babylon and Egypt where Jews lived in number. Little could any of those writers have known that Jerusalem would later become the center of three of the most significant religions on Earth.

There can be no doubt that Jewish leaders petitioned Cyrus for a return to Jerusalem. He didn't simply awake one day and think it a good idea to let the Jews go. That petition was made when Cyrus was distracted by the death of his beloved wife Cassandana. And it appears Cyrus limited the number who could return, and when—hence the spasmodic return over many years. As for Cyrus also decreeing permission for the reconstruction of the Temple, there is no evidence of that outside of Jewish sources. If any ruler should be credited with allowing construction of the Second Temple, it should be Darius. And he was distracted at the time by the aftermath of widespread rebellions, was keen to be seen to emulate Cyrus, and may well have been misled by a forged Cyrus decree or by advice from a Jewish subordinate such as Mordecai that such a decree existed when it didn't.

All in all, despite the fact that most of the wise words and acts credited to Cyrus by Xenophon in his influential *Cyropaedia* are likely to be false, and the fact that credit given to Cyrus in the Bible for allowing the Temple to be rebuilt may be misplaced, as a figure who dramatically changed history and ruled in a uniquely magnanimous way, Cyrus still deserves the title Great.

Cyrus is on record claiming to have been chosen by his "Lord of the heavens" to liberate and lead his people. Until recently, Donald Trump had not made such an assertion, allowing others to make the claim on his behalf. But then, in August 2019, while on the

White House lawns talking to the media about his trade war with China, President Trump looked to the heavens and declared, "I am the chosen one."[89] It would seem that he may have come to believe the heady comparison with Cyrus after all. However, as Professor Richter explains in the Afterword, that comparison has no historical credibility.

In the end, Cyrus, as great and wise a man as he was, proved fallible and perished after misjudging an opponent—a woman. It can only be wondered if history will repeat itself.

AFTERWORD

by Dr. David H. Richter, Ph.D.,

*Professor Emeritus of English and Comparative Literature, Queens
College and CUNY Doctoral Center, City University of New York*

1. CYRUS THE MEME

When my literary agent friend Richard Curtis told me that one
of his authors was working on a biography of Cyrus the Great,
I was interested, but skeptical about how much current interest
there would be in a Persian emperor who conquered the eastern
Mediterranean more than 2,500 years ago. "You would be surprised," he said. "Google 'Trump Cyrus' and you will see." When
I got home I did just that: there were nearly 53 million hits. Just
to check on whether you could pair the name Trump with any
conqueror of the sixth century BC and come up with gazillions of
Google hits, I tried "Trump Nebuchadnezzar" and came up with
less than 200,000—quite a few, but a different order of magnitude.
Evidently Trump/Cyrus was a meme. But what did that meme sig-
nify, and to whom and why?

Many of the websites that associated Donald Trump with
Cyrus the Great belonged to evangelical Christian ministers and

organizations who had supported Trump in the 2016 election, some quite reluctantly, not only because of Trump's scandalous sexual behavior, but because he seemed a Christian in name only, with no active connection to any church, and with no evidence that he had ever read the Bible, much less understood or followed its dictates.

Packaging a vote for Trump as the godly choice would be difficult. And one specimen public sermon supporting this view—it was not the first and it may not have been the ninety-first—was by Derek Thomas of First Presbyterian Church in Columbia, South Carolina. Thomas's sermon was delivered on October 16, 2016, just a week after the *Access Hollywood* tapes were made public, and its topic was Cyrus the Great. Thomas first cites the passage in Isaiah 45 that directly addressed Cyrus, then goes on to explain the place of Cyrus in biblical history:

> Cyrus was the first king of Persia who overthrew the kingdom of Babylon and destroyed the last king of Babylon, Nabonidus, in 539 BC. It's what is recorded in the opening verses of the book of Ezra that Cyrus issued a decree. Having conquered ancient Babylon, he issued a decree that those held in captivity in the Babylonian Empire and in Babylon itself were allowed to go back home—not just Jews, there were others too, but the Jews in particular. The Jews were freed to return to Judea, where over several decades they rebuilt the Temple and the wall around Jerusalem and reinstated their worship of the Lord.[90]

Cyrus ended the Israelites' captivity in Babylon, but that does not mean, for Thomas, that he was a good man; Cyrus was chosen by God to perform God's work, but that did not mean, for Thomas, that he was a godly man. Thomas in fact calls him "despot"; he calls him "dictator"; and indeed he calls him "a brute." The crucial passage in the sermon then follows:

> I don't think that you would have liked Cyrus. He did a wonderful thing, he did an extraordinary thing, God used him in the advancement of his kingdom, but I don't think that you'd have liked Cyrus the Great. So I

was thinking,... would you vote for Cyrus? I know I'm setting the cat among the pigeons here, but would you vote for Cyrus the Great...? God did. That's the issue. God voted for Cyrus. God employed Cyrus. God said yes to this man, this brute of a man. I'm just saying, as they say....

Isaiah is writing this about an event that is 200 years in Isaiah's future.... [What if] you were able to write an email suggesting what may take place 200 years from now and not just in vague general terms, but in specific detail that you could name the man in charge 200 years from now. Imagine that. I don't even know who's going to be in charge three weeks from now.[91]

"Three weeks from now" for Derek Thomas's audience, both in his church and online where his sermons were widely distributed, would be the election of 2016. By asking "would you vote for Cyrus?" Thomas in effect was calling for his flock to vote for a different "brute of a man" who nevertheless might very well be the crude and unworthy vessel through whom God's kingdom could be advanced. Donald Trump's name does not appear even once in this sermon—Thomas was perhaps aware that the special tax status of his church could be endangered if he endorsed political candidates—but he is clearly telling his listeners that an ungodly man can still be the man God chooses to do His work.

Thomas's argument—that Donald Trump might well be a latter-day Cyrus—was then taken up and brought into the right-wing propaganda echo chamber by Jerome Corsi, the fringe journalist and conspiracy theorist, then senior staff writer at *WorldNetDaily*. Corsi summarized Thomas's sermon in a lengthy article on October 18, with a lead beginning: "A movement is sweeping quietly across evangelical Christian America...."[92]

And Corsi was right about this: Cyrus was indeed becoming a meme. In fact a considerably earlier political tract appealing to the Cyrus meme by J. D. Edwards was called *The Cyrus Test: A Biblical Approach to Voting When Candidates Don't Share Your Faith* (2012). This 57-page e-book, still listed with Amazon, was published in

2012 just before Election Day. Edwards sought an answer for how to choose between Mitt Romney, a member of the Mormon church whose theology is an abomination to born-again evangelicals, and Barack Obama, a member of the evangelical United Church of Christ who nevertheless supported social policies like gay marriage and a woman's right to choose abortion, which are anathema to many born-again evangelicals. Edwards came up with what he called the Cyrus test—that the believing Christian should choose to be ruled by a "pagan" who shares your values over a "professed Christian" whose social values you oppose. Edwards's book long preceded Trump's candidacy, but of course Trump's scandal-filled private life would create considerably sharper dilemmas for evangelicals than Romney's Mormonism did.

At least three other books developed at considerably greater length Derek Thomas's notion that, like Cyrus the Great, Donald Trump had been chosen by God for His own "salvational" purpose, to reset America against all forms of "political correctness" and return it to traditional marriage and the sanctity of fetal life. Lance Wallnau, a motivational speaker and televangelist, published *God's Chaos Candidate: Donald J. Trump and the American Unraveling* (Keller, TX: Killer Sheep Media, 2016) on September 30, about two weeks before Derek Thomas's sermon. The following year, Jose De La Rosa published *Trump: The US's King Cyrus and the American Prayer* (Buford, GA: Faith Publishers, 2017). And in 2018, Greg Badalian published *Millennia: The Cyrus Key to the Donald Trump Presidency* (Leitchfield, KY: Lion of Zion Ministries, 2018). The Amazon blurb for Badalian's book suggests that the Cyrus meme had by then been taken up by evangelists who prophesy from their own dream-visions and those of their relatives:

> Before Greg's father died of cancer in 2014, he… had a dream that… veiled the next President, for in taking place in Persia, it tells of Trump as being a pattern of Cyrus.… Join Greg on a journey, to find the Last Trump, the Millennium and the New Jerusalem, as prefigured through

Donald Trump, his wife Melania and in his many luxurious resorts, but not for his glory, but for the glory of God, who encodes the latest, breaking news in the Bible!

2. FROM MEME TO MEDAL

If the Cyrus meme helped to elect Trump and to reaffirm his support among evangelical Christians, Trump's own actions as president have encouraged this identification. Most important among these has been Trump's recognition of Jerusalem as the capital of the State of Israel, and his moving the American embassy to West Jerusalem from Tel Aviv. On March 5, 2018, Israeli president Benjamin Netanyahu spoke from the Oval Office on the historic nature of Trump's action:

> I want to tell you that the Jewish people have a long memory. So we remember the proclamation of the great King Cyrus the Great—Persian king. Twenty-five hundred years ago, he proclaimed that the Jewish exiles in Babylon can come back and rebuild our temple in Jerusalem. We remember, one hundred years ago, Lord Balfour, who issued the Balfour Proclamation that recognized the rights of the Jewish people in our ancestral homeland. We remember fifty years ago, President Harry S. Truman was the first leader to recognize the Jewish state. And we remember how a few weeks ago, President Donald J. Trump recognized Jerusalem as Israel's capital. Mr. President, this will be remembered by our people throughout the ages. And as you just said, others talked about it. You did it. So I want to thank you on behalf of the people of Israel.[93]

Netanyahu drew a through-line from Cyrus to Trump via the Balfour Declaration promising a Jewish homeland in the Middle East and the United Nations' vote creating the State of Israel. The previous week, the Mikdash Educational Center on Jaffa Street in Jerusalem had announced that it had minted a coin—a Temple half-shekel in fact—commemorating Trump's action, which it would send to donors for a minimum donation of fifty dollars. Mikdash is an organization devoted to a program of restoring the

Jerusalem Temple on its original site on Temple Mount and training priests to perform the traditional sacrifices.

Not to be outdone by the Israelis, Lance Wallnau created his own Trump/Cyrus coin, which was marketed on disgraced televangelist Jim Bakker's program. Wallnau is underselling Mikdash, selling his coin for $45, although he also has a $450 package deal delivering thirteen sets consisting of a Trump/Cyrus coin and a booklet with thirteen prophecies concerning the reign of Donald Trump and its parallels in ancient Israelite history.

And Trump himself has brandished his identification with Cyrus in his own communications. In his first greeting to the Iranian people in 2017 on the occasion of Nowruz (the Iranian New Year, celebrated at the beginning of spring) he said, in part: "Cyrus the Great, a leader of the ancient Persian Empire, famously said that 'freedom, dignity, and wealth together constitute the greatest happiness of humanity. If you bequeath all three to your people, their love for you will never die.' To the Iranian people and all those around the world celebrating Nowruz: On behalf of the American people, I wish you freedom, dignity, and wealth."[94] Unfortunately Cyrus never actually said any such thing; the quotation comes from Larry Hedrick's 2006 how-to book *Xenophon's Cyrus the Great: The Arts of Leadership and War*, which re-creates Cyrus as a modern corporate CEO.

At this point it should be clear that the identification of Donald Trump with Cyrus the Great is a Looney Tunes fantasy by evangelical preachers and laymen designed to justify their political support for a leader whose moral character, actions, and language could not be further from the ideals that Jesus preached and Christianity professes. We need to come back to realities. The historical reality of Cyrus the Great, his character and career—and whether he actually was a dictator, a despot, and a brute, as the evangelicals suggest—you will have learned from Stephen Dando-Collins's biography. The other reality that we should examine briefly here is the difference between the way evangelicals read the references to Cyrus that appear in the books of Isaiah, Ezra, Nehemiah, Chronicles, and Daniel, and the way contemporary biblical scholars read them. The issues include the place of Cyrus in the history of Israel, along with what it would have meant for Isaiah to represent God calling Cyrus the Great "My anointed."

3. THE TWO (OR THREE) ISAIAHS

Derek Thomas is deeply impressed, astonished in fact, that Isaiah was able to predict the accession of Cyrus the Great to the position of absolute monarch over most of the ancient Near East more than two hundred years after the period when Isaiah lived. Of course, prophets are divinely inspired, so there can be no certain limits to their foreknowledge. But, except in certain fundamentalist circles, it is well understood that the book of Isaiah is a composite text with more than one author.[95]

The first thirty-nine chapters of Isaiah, or most of them, are clearly set in the late eighth century BC, written by Isaiah the son of Amoz, who was a first cousin of Hezekiah king of Judah. This Isaiah casually wanders in and out of Hezekiah's palace advising the king about how to handle the danger posed to his kingdom by the Assyrian Empire, which in 722 BC had destroyed the Northern Kingdom of Israel and dispersed its population, which became the "ten lost tribes." This Isaiah warns Hezekiah to trust in the LORD, rather than attempting to acquire cavalry from Egypt. At the end of these chapters, Isaiah's advice is vindicated. The Assyrian general Sennacherib besieges Jerusalem in 701 BC, and Hezekiah following Isaiah prays for deliverance. The Assyrian army is subsequently destroyed by a plague sent by an angel of the LORD; the siege is lifted and the kingdom and its capital are saved.

But starting at chapter 40, we find ourselves in a very different world. The kingdom of Judah no longer exists, the Davidic line of kings seems to be extinct. The community of Israelites is living in exile, and it is politically inert. Jerusalem and the Temple seem to have been destroyed. This Isaiah predicts a restoration, not of the Davidic kingdom, but of Judah and Jerusalem. This Isaiah predicts a return from exile, and he foresees that the Temple that had been destroyed by the Babylonians will be rebuilt. This Isaiah sees the agent of this restoration as Cyrus of Persia, who has recently conquered the empire of Babylonia. No one from the eighth century, neither Isaiah the son of Amoz nor any of his contemporaries, could have possibly understood this discourse, because it references conquerors like Cyrus and empires—Babylonia and Persia—that had not yet come into existence, but which the biblical text of Isaiah 40-66 simply takes for granted without any explanation.

Historical scholars are firmly convinced that the solution to this anomaly is that there was an anonymous prophet writing in the second half of the sixth century BC whose prophecies were appended to those of the eighth-century Isaiah. This prophet is referred to as "Second Isaiah." Some scholars view the last eleven chapters of Isaiah as the work of a still later writer or school of writers ("Third Isaiah") with somewhat different concerns and prophetic message than Second Isaiah. Where Second Isaiah looks forward to the return to Judea from exile and the reinstatement of the Temple cult, Third Isaiah preaches about the decline of ethical standards within Judea and the empty performance of ritual worship in place of moral behavior and charity to the poor.

4. THE THEOLOGY OF THE CALL OF CYRUS

Second Isaiah's Call of Cyrus—and it is not prose but an ecstatic poem—runs from the end of chapter 44 to the middle of chapter 45: Here is the full text in the JPS translation:

> Shout, O heavens, for the LORD has acted;
> Shout aloud, O depths of the earth!

Shout for joy, O mountains,
O forests with all your trees!
For the LORD has redeemed Jacob,
Has glorified Himself through Israel.

Thus said the LORD, your Redeemer,
Who formed you in the womb:
It is I, the LORD, who made everything,
Who alone stretched out the heavens
And unaided spread out the earth;

Who annul the omens of diviners,
And make fools of the augurs;
Who turn sages back
And make nonsense of their knowledge;

But confirm the word of My servant
And fulfill the prediction of My messengers.
It is I who say of Jerusalem, "It shall be inhabited,"
And of the towns of Judah, "They shall be rebuilt;
And I will restore their ruined places."

Who said to the deep, "Be dry;
I will dry up your floods,"

I am the same who says of Cyrus, "He is My shepherd;
He shall fulfill all My purposes!"
He shall say of Jerusalem, "She shall be rebuilt,"
And to the Temple: "You shall be founded again."

Thus said the LORD to Cyrus, His anointed one—
Whose right hand He has grasped,
Treading down nations before him,
Ungirding the loins of kings,
Opening doors before him
And letting no gate stay shut:

I will march before you
And level the hills that loom up;
I will shatter doors of bronze

And cut down iron bars.

I will give you treasures concealed in the dark and secret hoards—
So that you may know that it is I the LORD,
The God of Israel, who call you by name.

For the sake of My servant Jacob,
Israel My chosen one,
I call you by name,
I hail you by title, though you have not known Me.

I am the LORD and there is none else;
Beside Me, there is no god.
I engird you, though you have not known Me,

So that they may know, from east to west,
That there is none but Me.
I am the LORD and there is none else,

I form light and create darkness,
I make well-being and create evil—
I the LORD do all these things. (44:23–45:7)

Before we get to the LORD's address to Cyrus, calling Cyrus his "anointed one" and his "shepherd," we need to notice something unusual about the LORD's description of his own divine nature in this passage. In earlier biblical texts, the LORD had described himself as the greatest and most powerful god around, but nevertheless one of a population of divine beings. As He says to Moses in Exodus 12:12, "I will mete out punishments to all the gods of Egypt, I am the LORD." In the Song of the Sea in Exodus 15, the Israelites sing, "Who is like thee, LORD, among the gods, glorious in holiness, fearful in praises, doing wonders?" In the Ten Commandments, God tells the Israelites not to worship "any other gods besides Me." Apparently there were other gods.

The God of Second Isaiah still has a special relationship to the Israelites, but He can be no longer a merely national god, not merely because He is the greatest but because He is the only god there

is: "There is none but Me. I am the LORD and there is none else."
The implication is that, although Cyrus may not have "known"
the LORD by name, any notion of transcendent divinity he had
been able to conceive must have been about the LORD, who "alone
stretched out the heavens/ And unaided spread out the earth."
And one is tempted to think that the last line of Second Isaiah's
evocation of divinity—"I form light and create darkness..."—might
have been designed to appeal specifically to Persian Zoroastrians,
worshippers of Ahuramazda the lord of light—and that it is possible Cyrus was one of them, although biographer Dando-Collins
doubts this is the case.

5. CYRUS THE MESSIAH

For anyone reading Second Isaiah in Hebrew the most startling
phrase comes at the very beginning of chapter 45, in which the
prophet speaks of Cyrus as *meshicho*—God's "anointed one."
What exactly does that mean? The Hebrew word *mashiach* comes
from a fairly common verb *mashach* meaning to smear or spread
with a liquid, usually oil. The verb and its derived noun are used
about a hundred times in the Hebrew Bible in a variety of con-
texts. In Exodus 28, Moses is told that when he consecrates Aaron
and Aaron's sons as priests, they are to be anointed with a special
scented oil, and it is specified later that this will be done to all their
successors.[96] Prophets as well as priests can be anointed: in 1 Kings
19:16 Elijah is instructed to anoint Elisha as his successor.

In the historical books of the Hebrew Bible, "the anointed"
usually refers to a king of Israel. In 1 Samuel 9, the LORD tells the
prophet Samuel to anoint Saul to be the first king over all the Israelites, and in the following chapter he does so. In 1 Samuel 16,
after Saul has failed in his duties, Samuel anoints David to become
Saul's successor, although Saul remains king of Israel for many
years thereafter. In his old age, David has Solomon anointed by

Zadok the priest as a way of settling the succession of the throne. Thus kings as well as priests are anointed as part of their ceremony of investiture, a custom that modern European monarchies have adopted to this day. The scented anointing oil links the monarch's status to divinity, making his kingship sacred, his body sacrosanct. While on the run from Saul, David had several chances to kill him, but he refrained because Saul was "the LORD's anointed," and after Saul's death at the battle of Mount Gilboa, David had an Amalekite executed who claimed to have helped the gravely wounded king to commit suicide, because he dared "to touch the LORD's anointed."[97]

In a daring but not wholly unprecedented shift of reference, Second Isaiah applies this term "the LORD's anointed" to Cyrus. Cyrus is certainly not an Israelite, he may not be a believer in the LORD, but the LORD has chosen him anyway, has made Cyrus successful in battle and in political maneuvering in order to "fulfill all My purposes." Those "purposes" are to end the captivity of the Israelites in Babylonia and send them back to reinhabit Jerusalem and rebuild the holy temple that had been destroyed by Nebuchadnezzar in 586 BC. Possibly Second Isaiah hoped that his prophecy would get back to Cyrus and introduce him to the God of Israel who had assisted his conquests. But it is more likely that the intended audience was the Israelites in Babylon, who were being instructed to view Cyrus as their divinely ordained ruler, the one whose edicts would restore the nation of Israel and the national religion—although not the Davidic monarchy.

Along with "the anointed one," Second Isaiah calls Cyrus the LORD's "shepherd" at 44:28, a somewhat less frequent metaphor for a divinely approved secular ruler. The term first shows up in Numbers 27:17, when the aging Moses asked God to appoint Joshua to rule over the Israelites "that the congregation of the LORD be not as sheep which have no shepherd." In 2 Samuel 5, when the Israelites offered the monarchy to David, they told him "the LORD said to you 'You shall shepherd my people Israel'"—after which they anointed him as their king. (David had actually worked as a shepherd in his youth, of course.) And the prophets Jeremiah and Ezekiel both refer to the last Israelite kings and their counselors as evil shepherds who "rebel against Me" or who fail to tend their flocks.[98] Cyrus, to the contrary, will be the LORD's chosen shepherd, guiding the flock of Israel to its natural homeland and protecting it from its enemies.

Five centuries after Second Isaiah, the Hebrew term *mashiach*—the usual transliteration is "messiah"—came to be used in a very different sense, to denote "a charismatically endowed descendant of King David who the Jews of the Roman period believed would be raised up by God to break the yoke of the heathen and reign over a restored kingdom of Israel to which all the Jews of the Exile would return."[99] And of course the adjective "anointed" in its Greek form (*christos*) came to be used in a third sense, primarily by Paul but also by the evangelists in the New Testament, as an epithet for Jesus as the heavenly king whose second coming will herald the end of days. Rabbinic Judaism in the Talmud picked up this third sense of messiah, minus any specific application to Jesus of Nazareth, as the eschatological king who will preside over the world to come.

Although Second Isaiah means to say that Cyrus is a messiah in the earlier narrow sense of a divinely approved king, that is still a highly significant move. Whereas Isaiah the son of Amoz, the first Isaiah, had seen God as working wonders *within* history, personally sending an angel of death to destroy the Assyrian army, Second Isaiah sees God as working *through* history. God had punished the sins of Judah and Jerusalem by sending Nebuchadnezzar and the Babylonian army against them to destroy the Temple and the city, but now God had sent a savior in the form of Cyrus the Great, to restore Zion to its former glory. The Second Temple period that followed would be one of the most productive for the Israelites, for it was then that the Torah and the rest of the Hebrew Bible were written and edited: it was in that period that Judaism was essentially created. To be sure, the notion of a God who works through history would become problematic in the Roman period, when Jerusalem and the Temple were destroyed a second time, and it has become even more problematic in our own day, whenever we contemplate Hitler and the Holocaust.

6. CYRUS IN SECOND TEMPLE SCRIPTURE

In addition to Second Isaiah, Cyrus is mentioned in the biblical books of Ezra, Chronicles, and Daniel as the ruler who fulfilled, or at least began the fulfillment of, the divine purposes mentioned in Isaiah 44. The book of Ezra begins here:

> In the first year of King Cyrus of Persia, when the word of the LORD spoken by Jeremiah was fulfilled, the LORD roused the spirit of King Cyrus of Persia to issue a proclamation throughout his realm by word of mouth and in writing as follows: "Thus said King Cyrus of Persia: The LORD God of Heaven has given me all the kingdoms of the earth and has charged me with building Him a house in Jerusalem, which is in Judah. Any of you of all His people—may his God be with him—let him go up to Jerusalem that is in Judah and build the House of the LORD God of Israel, the God that is in Jerusalem; and all who stay behind, wherever he may be living, let the people of his place assist him with silver, gold, goods, and livestock, besides the freewill offering to the House of God that is in Jerusalem." So the chiefs of the clans of Judah and Benjamin, and the priests and Levites, all whose spirit had been roused by God, got ready to go up to build the House of the LORD that is in Jerusalem. All their neighbors supported them with silver vessels, with gold, with goods, with livestock, and with precious objects, besides what had been given as a freewill offering. King Cyrus of Persia released the vessels of the LORD's house which Nebuchadnezzar had taken away from Jerusalem and had put in the house of his god. (1:1–6)

A slightly different version of the first three verses is also used to conclude the books of Chronicles.

Cyrus's "first year" mentioned in Ezra is probably 539–538 BC, the year during which Cyrus overcame the Babylonian monarch

Nabonidus and began to rule from Babylon, where Israelite exiles were living. Ezra gives a partial list of those who returned enthusiastically from Babylon. The sacrificial cult was re-established almost immediately, but the rebuilding of Solomon's Temple under a new and enlarged plan did not go smoothly because the returning Israelites had enemies living in the land. It is not until the sixth year of the Persian emperor Darius, 516 BC, that the Second Temple said to be commanded by Cyrus was finally completed and dedicated.

The name of Cyrus appears also in the prophetic book of Daniel, but it is hard to know how seriously to take this because the chronology in that very late text has been jumbled badly. It is clear that, apart from some rulers' names, the author of Daniel had very little knowledge of or interest in the politics of the ancient Near East in the sixth century BC, and a great deal of interest in the politics of his own day. The character Daniel is an Israelite who was taken as a youth to Babylon in the first exile of 597 BC. There Daniel survived the reigns of Nebuchadnezzar and his son Belshazzar, after which Babylon was conquered by "Darius the Mede," who is supposed to be "the son of Ahasuerus" (i.e. Artaxerxes). Finally, Daniel lived into the reign of Cyrus, issuing his final prophecy in "the third year of the reign of Cyrus the Persian."

As you will have learned in the preceding biography of Cyrus, the important rulers of the Babylonian Empire in the sixth century were Nebuchadnezzar and Nabonidus, a usurper unrelated to his predecessor. Belshazzar was merely a son of Nabonidus, who served as governor of the city of Babylon until the Babylonian Empire was conquered by Cyrus in 539. As ruler of the enlarged Persian Empire, Cyrus was followed by his son Cambyses. After the death of Cambyses in 522, Darius I, a Persian nobleman only distantly related to Cyrus, became the emperor (522-487), followed by his son Xerxes I (487-465), who was followed by Xerxes's son Artaxerxes I (465-424). It is not easy to keep all this straight, but it is clear that the author of the book of Daniel did not bother to do so, calling Darius a Mede and introducing him as the son of Artaxerxes rather than his grandfather, and having Darius followed by Cyrus.

These complexities were of no interest to the author of Daniel, because the politics he was concerned about concerned the crisis that had begun in his own day, around 170 BC. The Persian Empire had faded into history because the Persians had lost direct control over the Jews of Israel and Judea after the Near East was conquered by Alexander the Great around 330 BC. After Alexander's death, his territories had been divided among his generals, including Ptolemy and his descendants, who ruled Egypt from Alexandria, and Seleucus and his descendants, who ruled Syria from the city of Antioch.

The Jews of Judea and Jerusalem lived quietly, paying taxes to the Ptolemies, until Seleucus's great-grandson Antiochus III conquered their territory. Antiochus III was tolerant of the Jews' religious practices, but his son and successor Antiochus IV ("Epiphanes") had very different ideas. His attempts to Hellenize the Jews and extirpate their traditional religious practices inspired the Maccabean revolt.

The book of Daniel, though set several centuries earlier, is filled with prophecies about a demonic "king of the north" (meaning Antiochus IV) who will make war on the "king of the south" (Ptolemy VI). During this war he will defile the Second Temple in Jerusalem by setting up within it "the abomination of desolation" (Daniel 11:31; this probably denotes a Greek altar to Zeus). This had actually happened in 167 BC. One response to this crisis was by the Maccabees, who took arms against the Seleucids and attempted to achieve independence for the Israelites, in which they succeeded for about a century, until the hegemonic power of Rome made the independence of small states in the Near East impossible.

The response of the author of Daniel was exactly the opposite. Like Isaiah son of Amoz during the Assyrian invasion of Judah, the author of Daniel held the quietist belief that the Jews should pray to God faithfully hoping that He would settle the situation all by Himself. The Israelites later honored both sides of this controversy: the Maccabee warriors with the annual holiday of Hanukkah, celebrating their rededication of the Temple, the quietist author of Daniel by having his book accepted into the Hebrew Bible.

Post-biblical references to Cyrus are scattered throughout the Talmud and the Midrash, about which the editor of the *Encyclopaedia Judaica* generalizes that the Palestinian rabbis give "a rather favorable account of him, while the Babylonians censure him."[100] In fact the historical Cyrus usually gets lost in a muddle of argumentation. In the tractate Rosh Hashanah at 3b, for example, various rabbis debate whether Cyrus, Darius, and Artaxerxes were virtuous rulers, after which the sixth-century redactor of the Talmud settles the matter by mashing all three emperors together: "The sages taught that... All three names are referring to the same person: He is Cyrus; he is Darius; and he is also Artaxerxes. He was called Cyrus because he was a virtuous [*kasher*] king; he was called Artaxerxes after his kingdom, i.e., this was his royal title; and what was his real name? Darius was his name."[101] Nevertheless, the name of Cyrus, like that of Alexander, is one that Jewish mothers often give to their sons; few other foreign conquerors have such a sweet-smelling reputation.

The reputation of Cyrus probably hit its high point from the Renaissance through the Enlightenment, owing to the accident that Xenophon's partly fictional biography of the Persian emperor, the *Cyropaedia*, came to be considered the ideal text for teaching the rudiments of classical Greek to British and European children. It influenced political thought and educational theory for at least three centuries, and Xenophon's vision of Cyrus as an ideal ruler was read enthusiastically or critically by political thinkers from Machiavelli to Montesquieu and Franklin, and spoofed in *Tristram Shandy* by Laurence Sterne. With the decline of classical Greek as the foundation for upper class education, Xenophon's biography fell in popularity, so that present-day evangelical preachers like Derek Thomas, apparently unaware of both the Hebrew and Greek traditions about Cyrus, could mistakenly call him "this brute of a man" and could view the Persian conqueror as a kindred spirit to contemporary brutes like Donald Trump.

ENDNOTES

INTRODUCTION: OUR SOURCES ON CYRUS

1. Xenophon, *Cyropaedia*, Amazon, 2018.
2. Plutarch and John Dryden, trans., *Plutarch's Lives*, "Artaxerxes."
3. Lloyd Llewellyn-Jones, *Ctesias's History of Persia: Tales of the Orient*.
4. Caro, PBS *Newshour*, April 8, 2019.

1. KILL THE CHILD

5. Aristotle, *On Prophesying by Dreams*.
6–11. Herodotus and John M. Marincola et al., *The Histories*.

2. DEPORTING THE JEWS TO BABYLON

12. Some historians contest the year this took place, suggesting 596 BC, not 597 BC.

3. THE BOY IN THE BASKET

13. Herodotus, in *The Histories*, refers here to Astyages as king of Media. However, we know that Astyages was still only the crown prince at this point. It would be another five years before he ascended his father's throne.

14. Herodotus.

4. SAVED BY THE MAGI

15. All the dialogue in this chapter is from Herodotus, *The Histories*.

16. Ctesias, in his version, called Cyrus's foster parents Atredates and Argoste, names which scholars dismiss.

6. IN THE COURT OF THE KING

17. Xenophon.

18. Ctesias/Nicolaus, *The Persica*. Ctesias also mentions a Babylonian priest who supposedly accompanied Cyrus on this trip and was murdered by Oebares. The Babylonian was possibly one of Ctesias's fictions.

7. LEADING THE PERSIAN REVOLT

19. Herodotus.

20. Ctesias, *The Persica*.

21. Ibid.

22. Ibid.

23. Ibid.

8. CYRUS'S FIRST BATTLE

24. Ctesias claims Cyrus and the townspeople had been joined for the battle by 1,500 cavalry and 5,000 infantry sent by King Cambyses, but as previously noted, this isn't credible. Besides, it's highly unlikely that the 300 Median troopers would have engaged in battle when so vastly outnumbered by 6,500 Persian troops, plus the armed townsmen.

25. Herodotus.

26. Ibid.

27. Ibid.

28. Ibid.

29. Ibid.

9. BATTLE OF THE BORDER

30. Ctesias.

31. Ibid.

32. Ibid.

10. BATTLE OF PASARGADAE: THE FALL OF ASTYAGES

33. Ctesias.

34. Ibid.

35. Herodotus.

36. Ctesias.

37. Herodotus.

11. A MIGHTY EMPIRE WILL BE DESTROYED

38. Plutarch, in his *Lives of the Noble Grecians and Romans* chapter on Solon, comments that some authors of his day doubted that the chronology of the lives of Croesus and Solon allowed them to actually meet. However, modern historians believe that Solon died in Delphi in 560 BC, the year Croesus came to the throne. This doesn't preclude the pair meeting in the short period between Croesus's ascent to the throne and Solon's death. Nor does it preclude the more likely scenario of Solon visiting Sardis earlier, when Croesus was crown prince and in charge at Sardis while his father was away on campaign against the Medes. Plutarch and Herodotus both believed the pair met and conversed in Sardis.

39. Herodotus.

40. Ibid.

12. CROESUS VERSUS CYRUS

41. See Stephen Dando-Collins, *Mark Antony's Heroes* and *Legions of Rome: The Definitive History of Every Imperial Roman Legion.*

42. Herodotus.

13. SARDIS: THE FALLEN HELMET

43. Herodotus.

44. Ibid.

45. Ibid.

46. Reinhold Bichler, "Ctesias 'Corrects' Herodotus." And Bichler, *Herodot*.

14. KILLING A KING

47. Herodotus.

48. Plutarch's "Solon" chapter. He also writes that Aesop, creator of *Aesop's Fables*, was present at Sardis during Solon's visit, while on the ancient equivalent of a lecture tour, and he scolded Solon for being rude to their host.

49. Herodotus.

50. Ibid.

51. Ibid.

52. Ibid.

53. Ibid.

54. Ibid.

15. FEET OF CLAY

55. The book of Daniel.

56. The Verse Account of Nabonidus.

57. Ibid.

58. Nabonidus Cylinder of Sippar.

59. Ibid.

60. Ibid.

16. MARCHING ON BABYLON

61. Nabonidus Chronicle.

62. Nabonidus Cylinder of Sippar.

63. Verse Account of Nabonidus.

64. Herodotus says a battle took place outside Babylon, but scholars generally agree this battle was the one at Opis, as attested by inscriptions.

17. THE WRITING IS ON THE WALL FOR NABONIDUS

65. The book of Daniel.

66. Cyrus Cylinder.

67. Ibid.

68. Verse Account of Nabonidus.

69. Cyrus Cylinder.

70. Verse Account of Nabonidus.

71. Cyrus Cylinder.

72. Ibid.

73. Jean Perrot, *The Palace of Darius at Susa: The Great Royal Residence of Achaemenid Persia*, "Darius the Great King."

74. Finkel, *The Cyrus Cylinder: The Great Persian Edict from Babylon.*

19. "DO NOT GRUDGE ME MY MONUMENT"

75. Arrian, *Anabasis of Alexander.*

20. THE SONS OF CYRUS

76. "Brain Tumor Overview," Harvard Health Publishing. www.health.harvard.edu/a_to_z/brain.tumor-overview-a-to-z.

77. We know Bardiya's name from Darius's Behistun Inscription. He was

called Smerdis by Herodotus and Tanyoxarces by Ctesias.

78. Herodotus.

79. Ibid.

80. Ibid.

81. Ibid.

21. DARIUS AND THE JERUSALEM TEMPLE

82. See Stephen Dando-Collins, *Rise of an Empire: How One Man United Greece to Defeat Xerxes's Persians.*

83. Bickerman, "The Babylonian Captivity," in Louis Finkelstein, *The Cambridge History of Judaism.* And Diana Vikander Edelman, *The Origins of the Second Temple.*

84. The book of Ezra.

EPILOGUE: WAS CYRUS GREAT? AND IS THERE A MODERN PARALLEL?

85. December 31, 2018.

86. *Times of Israel,* March 8, 2018.

87. Mike Evans on the Christian Broadcasting Network, quoted in *Times of Israel,* March 8, 2018.

88. Francois Vallat, in Perrot, *The Palace of Darius at Susa.*

89. CNN, August 21, 2019.

AFTERWORD

90. www.sermonaudio.com/fpcolumbia. Accessed June 19, 2019.

91. Ibid.

92. If Corsi's name seems familiar, it is because he was interrogated during the Mueller investigation of Russian interference in the 2016 election because of

his connections with then Trump aide Roger Stone, who was a go-between with Julian Assange at WikiLeaks. Corsi allegedly committed perjury during the interrogation and was sent a plea agreement, which he refused to sign. Despite this Mueller did not indict Corsi, for reasons that have not been explained. Corsi's conspiracy theories began with the "Swift Boat" attacks on the wartime heroism of Al Gore during the election of 2000; he was the author of the bestseller *Unfit to Command*. More recently he was the author of *Obama Nation* (2008).

93. *Times of Israel*, March 8, 2018.

94. https://ir.usembassy.gov/statement-president-trump-nowruz/

95. The composite character of the book of Isaiah—its having been written in the eighth and sixth centuries BC—was grasped by medieval Jewish biblical commentators like Abraham Ibn Ezra as early as the twelfth century, but the historical scholarship on Isaiah began with German Enlightenment scholarship in the late eighteenth century.

96. Inanimate objects are also anointed. We are told that parts of the tabernacle are to be anointed with scented oil on the day the sacrificial cult is inaugurated, and some of the crunchy loaves of shew-bread displayed in the tabernacle are also anointed, probably with ordinary olive oil.

97. David spared Saul in 1 Samuel 24 and 26; he had the Amalekite executed in 2 Samuel 1. Generally one would expect that the "anointed one" would be the legitimate reigning king of Israel, but as we learn in 2 Samuel 19:10, Absalom was anointed by his followers during his civil war against his father King David as a way of claiming legitimacy. And in 1 Kings 19, Elijah was told to anoint a Syrian, one Hazael, as king over Aram.

98. Jeremiah 2:8; Ezekiel 34:2-6.

99. Harold Louis Ginsberg, "Messiah" in *Encyclopaedia Judaica*, second edition volume 14, p. 110.

100. *Encyclopaedia Judaica*, second edition, vol 5, p. 351.

101. The Babylonian Talmud in the William Davidson translation, b. Rosh Hashanah 3b, retrieved from Sefaria.com.

BIBLIOGRAPHY

Books

Aristotle, *The Works of Aristotle, Book I,* Chicago: University of Chicago, 1989.

Arrian, *The Anabasis of Alexander: Or, the History of the Wars & Conquests of Alexander the Great.* London: Hodder & Stoughton, 1884.

Bichler, R., *Herodot.* Hildesheim: Georg Olnus Verlag, 2014.

Burstein, S.M., *The Babyloniaca of Berossus.* Undena: Malibu, 1978.

Ctesias, *History of Persia* (L. Llewellyn-Jones & J. Robson, eds.). Abingdon: Routledge, 2013.

Dando-Collins, S., *Legions of Rome.* London: Quercus, 2010.

Dando-Collins, S., *Mark Antony's Heroes: How the Third Gallica Legion Saved an Apostle and Created an Emperor.* Hoboken: Wiley, 2007.

Dando-Collins, S., *Rise of an Empire: How One Man United Greece to Defeat Xerxes's Persians.* Nashville: Wiley, 2013.

Edelman, D.V., *The Origins of the Second Temple: Persian Imperial Policy and the Rebuilding of Jerusalem.* Abingdon: Routledge, 2014.

Eusebius, *Chronicon.* Delhi: Pranava, 2018.

Farazmand, A. (ed.), *Handbook of Comparative and Development Public Administration.* New York: Marcel Dekker, 2001.

Finkel, I., *The Cyrus Cylinder: The Great Persian Edict from Babylon.* London: I.B. Tauris, 2013.

Finkelstein, L., *The Cambridge History of Judaism, Vol. 1*. Cambridge: Cambridge University Press, 1984.

Harrison, T., and E. Irwin, (eds.), *Interpreting Herodotus*. Oxford: Oxford University Press, 2018.

Hedrick, L., *Xenophon's Cyrus the Great: The Arts of Leadership and War*. New York: St. Martin's Griffin, 2007.

Herodotus, *The History of Herodotus*. Chicago, University of Chicago: 1989.

Holy Bible (King James Version). London: Collins, 1957.

Josephus F., *The New Complete Works of Josephus*, (W. Whiston transl.). Grand Rapids: Kregel, 1999.

Muller, K.O., (ed.), *Fragmenta Historicorum Graecorum, Vol. 3*. Greece: Didot, 1849.

Perrot, J., (ed.), *The Palace of Darius at Susa: The Great Royal Residence of Achaemenid Persia*. London: I.B. Tauris, 2013.

Plutarch, *The Lives of the Noble Grecians and Romans* (the Dryden translation). Chicago: University of Chicago, 1989.

Pritchard, J.B., *Ancient Near Eastern Texts Relating to the Old Testament*. Princeton: Princeton University, 1950.

Roth, C. (ed.), *Encyclopaedia Judaica*. New York: Macmillan, 1971.

Wells, H.G., *Outline of History, Vol. 1*. New York: Macmillan, 1921.

Xenophon, *Cyropaedia: The Education of Cyrus*. Marston Gate, Amazon, 2019.

Scholarly Articles

Bichler, R., "Ctesias 'Corrects' Herodotus: A Literary Assessment of the *Persica*." *Ad Fontes. Festschuft fur Gerhard Dobesch*, Vienna, 2004.

Cruz-Uribe, E., "Saite and Persian Demotic Cattle Documents: A Study in Legal Forms and Principles in Ancient Egypt." *American Studies in Papyrology*, 26, Chico, California, 1985.

Fried, L.S., "Cyrus the Messiah? The Historical Background to Isaiah 45:1." *Harvard Theological Review*, 95 (4), Harvard University, 2002.

NEWSPAPERS

New York Times, 2016-2019

Times of Israel, 2018-2019

OTHER

CNN, 2019

"Brain Tumor Overview," Harvard Health Publishing. www.health.harvard.edu/a_to_z/brain.tumor-overview-a-to-z

PBS *Newshour,* 2019

www.ir.usembasy.gov

www.sefaria.com

www.sermonaudio.com

INDEX

A

Access Hollywood, 190
Adad-Guppi, 116
Addagoppe, Queen, 116
Aegean Sea, 75, 166
Ahmadinejad, Mahmoud, 184
Akkadian language, 21, 110
Alexander the Great, 7–8, 158, 162, 186, 204
Alexander's death, 204
Amasis, Pharaoh, 126, 166–169
Amel-Marduk, 21, 115–116
Ammon, god, 170
Anabasis, 8
Antiochus III, 204
Antiochus IV, 204
Antony, Mark, 7, 81
Apries, Pharaoh, 34, 167
Araxes River, 159
Arrian, Lucius Flavius, 5, 8, 162
Artaxerxes II, 2, 4, 185
Ashpenaz, 110
Assyrian Empire, 144, 195
Astyages, 2, 12–17, 24–31, 38–48, 51–72, 105–106, 121, 153, 166
Atossa, daughter of Cyrus, 64, 164, 175, 178
Augustus, 7, 78

B

Babylon's Esagila Temple, 123
    power, 108
Babylonia, 8, 107–110, 122–125, 138–141, 146–149, 178, 196, 200
Babyloniaca, 8
Babylonian civil service, 110
Diaspora, 109
Badalian, Greg, 192
Bagapates, 70, 106, 162, 165
Battle of Babylon
    Hybra Pasargadae, 64, 70–71, 82, 89, 209
    Pteria Sardis, 103
    the Border
    the Eclipse
Belshazzar, Prince, 127, 130
Belteshazzar, 22, 110, 112, 137
Berossus, 7–8, 129, 132, 140–141
Bichler, Reinhold, 95
Bickerman, Elias, 179
Bilshan the Marduka, 181 Bilshan, Mordecai, 181
book of Ezra, 8, 149, 152, 179, 190, 202

C

Caesar, Julius, 54, 186
Caria, ix, 4, 79, 83, 86, 91, 101, 122

Carian military veterans, 83

Cassandana, Cyrus' wife, 43, 53, 61, 64, 69, 106, 155, 187

Christ, Jesus, 12, 158 Citadel of Babylon, 131

Corsi, Jerome, 191

Croesus, 5, 7–8, 105, 110, 125, 159–161, 166–169, 172–177

Croesus's army, 80, 82

Croesus, King, 5, 7, 75, 72–87, 90–103, 110, 125, 160, 168

Ctesias, 4–5, 53–54, 60–62, 65–66, 70–71, 93–94, 159–162, 168–169, 174–175

Cyaxares, 2, 11–12, 24–25, 37–38

Cyno, Cyrus' foster mother, 15–18, 32–33

Cyropaedia, 2–3, 162, 187, 205

Cyrus
  Edict of, 181, 184
  First Battle, 50, 208
  Persian Empire, 70
  possessions, 125
  Sons of, 165–176
  Cyrus II (Cyrus the Great), 6–10, 183–185, 189–195, 201
  'childhood,'
  'career under Astyages'
Cyrus Cylinder, 4, 9, 130, 140–141, 144–145, 153–154, 184

Cyrus the Messiah, 199

D
daggers, 58

Daniel, 8, 21, 109–116, 136–139, 146–149, 158, 195, 202–205

Darius the Mede, 146–147, 203

Darius, the Great, 69, 125–128, 146–150, 157–161, 165, 174–182, 186–187, 203–205

databara, 95, 169

De La Rosa, Jose, 192

Delphic Pythia, 74

Dido, Queen, 170

E
Ecbatana, Median capital, 5, 11–18, 23– 25, 31, 38-39, 42, 43, 45, 47, 48, 51–52, 66, 68, 69–70, 72, 77, 78, 80, 102–103, 105, 142, 154, 157, 178–179, 181

Edelman, Diana, 179 Edwards, J. D., 191 Encyclopaedia Judaica, 205

Elam, 108–109, 122, 124, 127, 142, 165, 178

Esther, 8, 181

Ethiopian Campaign, 170

Ezra, 8, 149–152, 155–157, 179–180, 190, 195, 202–203

F
Fallen Helmet, 89–95

G
Gedaliah, 35–36

Gediz River, 75

Gobryas, 127–129, 175

Golan Heights, 185

Gyndes River, 126–127

Gubara, governor, 128–129, 132, 134–135, 146–147

Gutium, 128, 144

H
Harpagus, 14–18, 26–30, 44–46, 53, 60, 62, 66–69, 103–105, 121–122, 125

Harran, 9, 108, 116, 118, 124, 145

Hebrew Bible, 199, 201, 205

Hedrick, Larry, 194

Herod the Great, 7, 181

Herodotus, 28, 32, 80, 85, 90, 93–96, 100

Hitler, 202

Holocaust, 202

Hophra, 34

Horses, sacred, 34–35, 41, 46, 126, 130,

Hystaspes, 84–85, 88, 92, 125, 147, 159–161, 165, 178

I
Imgur-Enlil Wall, 143

Immortals, 1, 58-59, 62, 78–79, 99, 124, 161, 168

Iona, ix
Ionian cities, 79, 101, 104–106
Ionian league, 105
Iranian Heritage Foundation, 186
Isaiah, 8, 21, 35, 153–154, 185, 190–191, 195–204
Ishtar Gate, 112, 123, 130, 132, 139
Islamic republic, 183

J
Jeconiah, 20–21, 115–116, 151
Jefferson, Thomas, 1–2
Jehoiakim, 19–20
Jeremiah, 8, 201–202
Jerusalem Temple, 156, 178–182, 194
Jewish, 1, 7–8, 19–21, 34–36, 108–112, 115, 149–156, 179, 185–187, 193, 205
Jewish Antiquities, 7–8, 149–150
Josephus, 7–8, 149–150, 152, 155, 174
Josephus, Flavius, 7

K
Karkheh River, 109
kasher, 205
kidaris, 59, 67
Kizilirmak River, 37

L
Labashi-Marduk, 111, 115
Lacedaemonians, 75, 101
Llewellyn-Jones, Lloyd, 5
Lord of the heavens, 21, 181, 187
Lydia, ix, 24–25, 37–38, 72, 75–76, 77, 79–80, 84, 86, 96, 103, 106, 122, 159
Lydian-Median treaty, 38

M
Machiavelli, Niccolò, 2
Mandana, 12–18, 26–28, 32, 38–39, 56, 63, 67–68
Marduk, 8, 9, 21, 33, 111–112, 115–120, 123–125, 129, 131–132, 134–135, 140–143, 145, 149, 152–153, 156, 186

Festival of, 112, 117, 119, 123, 125
mashach, 199
Mazares, Median general, 44, 57, 66, 67, 77, 98, 103–104
Median Empire, 11–13, 53, 74
Mehregan, 134
Memphis, Egyptian capital, xi, 83, 169, 171, 172,
meshicho, 199
Midrash, 205
Mighty Empire, 72
Mithradates, Cyrus' foster father, 15–18, 23–29, 31, 32, 153
Moses, 198–200
Mount Gilboa, 200

N
Nabu, god, 21, 73, 116, 123–124, 182
Nabonidus, 9, 66, 69–70, 111, 115–129, 136–145, 153, 155, 184, 190, 203
Nabonidus Cylinders, 9
Nabonidus's army, 119
Nabonidus, Verse Account of 66, 70, 119, 120, 141–145,
Nebuchadnezzar II, King, 1,9, 19, 34, 108–109
Negev Desert, 108, 167
Neo-Babylonian Empire, 108, 111
Netanyahu, Benjamin, 185, 193
Nicolaus, 6–7, 29, 38–40, 45
Nitetis, Princess, 167
Nitocris, Queen, 133, 137

O
Oebares, Cyrus' deputy, 5, 41–42, 46–49, 50, 56, 58, 61, 62, 65–68, 84, 91–95, 98, 105–106
Opis, xi, 108, 126–129, 134,

P
Pactolus River, 72
Pahlavi, Mohammad Reza, 183
Pasargadae, x, 4, 39, 47, 61–63, 82, 89, 105, 142, 162, 165, 178,–181, 183, 184

Peloponnese peninsula, 75
Percival, John, 3
Persian
    city, 47, 50, 58
    Empire, 1, 4, 10, 33, 70, 78, 124
    occupation, 112
    Revolt, 53, 77
    swords, 58
Persica, 4–5
Petisacas, chief eunuch, 40, 70, 105–106
Phoenicians, 170
Plutarch, 4, 7–8, 73
Prexaspes, 165–168, 172–173, 175
Psamtik III, Pharaoh, 168-169
Ptolemy VI, 204

R
Ramadan, 123
Richter, David H., 8, 154, 189 Roman
    chariot horses, 55 Roxane, 64, 164,
    168, 174–175

S
Sardis, Lydian capital, ix, 72–73, 86,
    88–95, 101–104,
Sardis's Temple, 93
satrapy, 78, 101, 121, 143, 147, 150, 156,
    158, 166, 178
scimitars, 58, 163
Second Isaiah, 196–202
Second Temple Scripture, 202
Shahbaz, 82, 90, 128
Shenazzar, 151
Shield Bearers, 131
Shushan, 109
Sippar, 9, 108, 118, 127, 129, 134, 145
Siwa Oasis, 170
Socrates, philosopher, 2
Solon of Athens, 73, 97
Sterne, Laurence, 205
Stewart, Katherine, 185
Susa, Elamite capital, ix, 20, 108–109, 122,
    124–125, 144, 157, 172, 174

T
Talmud, 8, 181–182, 201, 205
Tekel, 136, 138
Tema, Arabia, 119, 122, 125, 133, 141
Temple of Apollo, 8, 73, 75, 93
Tobit, Book of, 125
Tomyris, Queen of Massagetae, 159–162,
    166
    Ezida, 123
    Marduk, 117, 123
    Mount Gerizim, 156, 158
    Sardis, 172, 177
    Sin, 116–117, 119
Thales of Miletus, 38, 80
Thanes, 167–169
The Histories, 4–6
The Outline of History, 9, 132
The Trump Prophecy, 185
Third Isaiah, 196
Thomas, Derek, 190–192, 195, 206
Tigris River, 126, 184
Tristram Shandy, 205
Trojan chariot, 54
Trojan War, 6
Trump, Donald, 184–194, 206

V
vacabara, 173

W
Wallnau, Lance, 192, 194
Wells, H. G., 9, 132
WorldNetDaily, 191

X
Xenophon, 2–4, 38–40, 81–85, 91–92,
    101–102, 124–135, 138–139, 142–143,
    205–206
Xenophon's book, 2–3
Xerxes, 147, 178, 203

Z
Zagros Mountains, 14, 127
Zedekiah, 20, 34–35

CPSIA information can be obtained
at www.ICGtesting.com
Printed in the USA
JSHW031111060720
6525JS00001B/38